ALIEN LANDSCAPES

ALIEN LANDSCAPES

Robert Holdstock   Malcolm Edwards

MAYFLOWER BOOKS
NEW YORK

Copyright (Text) 1979 by Malcolm Edwards & Robert Holdstock
Copyright (Illustrations) 1979 by Young Artists

All rights reserved under International and
Pan American Copyright Convention.
Published in the United States by
Mayflower Books, Inc, New York City 10022.
Originally published in England by
Pierrot Publishing Limited, London.

Designed by Peter Gladwin

No part of this publication may be
reproduced, stored in a retrieval system, or
transmitted, in any form or by any means,
without prior written permission of the
publishers. Inquiries should be addressed to
Mayflower Books, Inc.

Library of Congress Cataloging in Publication Data
Alien Landscapes
1. Science Fiction – Illustrations
I Edwards, Malcolm II Holdstock, Robert
NC961.7.S34A43 808.83'876
79 – 13431
ISBN: 0 8317 0285 0

Manufactured in Italy

First American edition

CONTENTS

Introduction

Alienness is central to science fiction. Open practically any sf novel and somewhere on the page will be the descriptive hints or behavioural anomalies which indicate the presence of the alien. The characters may appear normal, speaking and acting in comprehensible and acceptable ways, but it will soon emerge that they are doing these things against a background which is anything *but* normal. Certainly there are exceptions – Thomas M. Disch's *334* is an excellent example – sf stories which deal with recognizable characters in familiar settings (New York a few decades hence in the case of Disch's novel). But the vast majority of sf stories take place in fantastic locations, or bring fantastic happenings to familiar places. Sf worlds are *strange* worlds. Earth is transformed by cataclysm, or by the slow processes of time; ordinary lives are disrupted by the arrival of alien visitors; pioneers explore exotic planets beneath distant suns. This book looks at a few of the wonderful alien landscapes to be found in the pages of modern science fiction.

The idea of visiting other worlds is almost as old as the idea that there are other worlds to visit. The first fictional account of a trip to the Moon dates from the second century A.D. There followed a hiatus lasting more than a thousand years, but by the 19th century accounts of journeys to the Moon or Mars or Venus were becoming quite common. What the travellers found on arrival, however, was not generally much different from what they had left behind them. The stories set in these displaced terrestrial locations were satirical or utopian – representatives of schools of fiction which had become well established since the publication of Thomas More's *Utopia* and Jonathan Swift's *Gulliver's Travels* in, respectively, the early 16th and early 18th centuries. In More's book a traveller returns from a distant island – Utopia – with an account of the perfect society devised by its inhabitants; in Swift's, a series of fantastic locations – a society of midgets, a land of giants, a floating island, and so forth – provide the setting for the author's scathing commentary on his own society.

Had they been writing in the 1970s, More and Swift might have set their works on other worlds. But until the early part of the twentieth century there were still enough blank spaces on the map for authors to imagine whatever societies they liked. As Western man went about his so-called discovery of distant parts of the globe (most of which were already perfectly well known to their inhabitants), this became more difficult. Still, it remained possible for H. Rider Haggard – and many imitators – to uncover an ancient civilization in a lost African valley (*She*, 1887) or for Sir Arthur Conan Doyle to invent a remote South American plateau inhabited by an enclave of prehistoric monsters (*The Lost World,* 1912). Indeed, the 'lost race' story became a popular subgenre of its own in the early part of this century, with *King Kong* and *Lost Horizon* – thanks to the silver screen – being among its most popular manifestations.

One school of science fiction simply uprooted these exotic locales for romantic adventure and transported them bodily to other planets. Mars and Venus, in particular, became the new frontiers. The accepted picture of Mars around the turn of the century was that popularized by astronomers Lowell and Schiaparelli – an ageing world, with greenish patches indicating vegetation, clearly visible icecaps, and the famous network of 'canals' (a mistranslation which immediately seized the popular imagination). Venus, conversely, was a young world, shrouded in cloud, its surface wet and humid. Both planets were assumed to have breathable atmospheres (there was then no reason to suppose otherwise). The greatest exponent of such adventures was Edgar Rice Burroughs, the first of whose Martian novels appeared in 1912. Burroughs concocted an exotic mix of stately palaces and beautiful princesses, villains of unsurpassed evil, strange flora and fauna, and headlong adventure. (He was also a master of cliffhanging endings to his novels, thus ensuring an eager audience for each sequel.)

This type of story is sometimes called science fantasy, although it contains no apparent science. The stories are first and foremost, adventures. The setting provides colour, and allows the author's imagination full rein, but it is not to be taken seriously. These are never-never lands, and as our knowledge of the solar system increases they are banished deeper into the galaxy, or into the imaginary Earths of the sword-and-sorcery fantasy. The work of Leigh Brackett – perhaps the most successful writer in the Burroughsian mould – provides a clear example. Up until the early 1950s she was still able to write of Mars as an ancient, exotic, decadent world, chiefly in her chronicles of the adventurer Eric John Stark. Returning to Stark in the 1970s, after a twenty year absence, she found it necessary to relocate him on a distant planet of another star, where anything is still theoretically possible. Other writers, such as Marion Zimmer Bradley in her popular Darkover series, produced similar science fantasy adventures. At their worst, such stories merely transported the Wild West or oriental adventure to other planets; in the hands of authors like Brackett and Bradley, the level of invention and imagination made the format distinctive and rewarding in its own right.

We also encounter invented worlds in pure fantasy, and it is often hard to draw a distinction between fantasy and sf settings. For instance, Andre Norton's Witch World series has a framing device which is clearly science-fictional, although the adventures are straightforward fantasy, complete with wizards and magic; conversely, Anne McCaffrey's Dragonrider stories take a situation of fantasy-adventure (giant fire-breathing dragons, and their riders) and place it in a carefully-rationalized science fiction context. There is no clear borderline. It is a general tendency of fantasy worlds – no doubt partly in imitation of *Lord of the Rings* – to be mapped in some detail, whereas most sf worlds are far more inexact geographically (Arrakis and Pern are exceptions to this generalization). Part of the reason for this may be that the fantasy worlds are similar to Earth in most minor details, the difference being the introduction of various elements from myth and legend. Characters ride horses across meadows towards stone castles, even though they may be waylaid *en route* by trolls, or goblins, or sorcerers. Therefore the world needs a precise physical outline to differentiate it from our own world.

Science fiction worlds, on the other hand, are more than just settings for fantastic adventure. They may, in a sense, be the central characters of the story. Some science fiction writers and critics claim, generally rather defensively, that sf cannot be judged by normal literary criteria because the *idea* is the hero of the story, and normal literary criticism is not equipped to deal with such works. As a general case this is not convincing, but certainly such locations as Mesklin, Ringworld, Arrakis and Rama are to a large degree the stars of their respective stories. Sf worlds may also function symbolically – as, for example, in Ursula Le Guin's *The Dispossessed*, where the twin worlds of Urras and Anarres, the one bounteous and the other arid, relate to and emphasize the respectively exploitative and ascetic nature of their societies – or as objective correlatives, giving physical expression to ideas or psychological states. They may become testing grounds for the struggle of mankind against its environment, or demonstrations of humanity's place and relative importance in the larger Universe. Science fiction settings will have a clear enough general location – usually light years from the solar system – and differing physical conditions: it is these, rather than precise geographical conditions, which typically concern us. The variety of alien landscapes is immense, and cannot readily be classified. Nevertheless we can identify a few important recurring patterns.

Extremes of Earth One method of devising an alien world (and also the inspiration for

12,000 M — Sun going cold
Shrinking to white dwarf

Red cold – Life on earth mainly
giant crabs and butterflies

11,000 M

Red warm – Jungle and forest
stasis for many billions of years

End of hydrogen – burning phase of sun   10,000 M — Sun turns red

Age of botanic reassertion
man reduced to one species

Stone building man – mile high city built around earth

High technology re-achieved and destroyed cyclically

Stone building man   9,000 M

Long age of devolution of man – withdrawal to less than 1000
worlds. All interworld contact lost in first million years –
nine major changes in man on earth

8,000 M

3rd sequence of galactic empires
– earth a revered shrine, much colonized

First resettlement by Intergalactic Man

Age of neo-insects

Unexplained disappearance of human life from earth

7,000 M

2nd interregnum – solar system taboo to Galactic man,
then forgotten as galactic empires war with each other
and are destroyed. Magic replaces science on earth

Solar flare destroys most life on earth   6,000 M — Second great sequence of solar empires – new Galactic League

Recolonization of earth from polar caps outwards

Interregnum: man not on earth (500 million years)

Man on earth

Age of dinosaurs (100 million years)   5,000 M

First trees
First fossil life laid down in abundance

First life on land

4,000 M

3,000 M

2,000 M — Life begins – single celled animals

1,000 M

FORMATION OF EARTH
FORMATION OF SUN

SUN FROM BIRTH TO DEATH
(12 Thousand million years of sun)

Galactic Time Chart

1 MILLION BC – 1 MILLION AD

1 Million AD Earth forgotten by Galactic man

Age of ghosts

Passing of eloi 900,000 AD Earth deserted

Expedition to earth 800,000 AD Extinction of morlocks
ifies galactic command
Earth declared forbidden zone

700,000 AD Rise of morlocks – man divided into two sub species – eloi above ground, morlocks below

inning of re-contact by 600,000 AD Complete trade co-operation re-established in galaxy
sts from other galaxies

500,000 AD Fall of empire – galaxy enters 100,000 years of primitivism – The silent stars

The bright galaxy
– empire prosperity 400,000 AD Invasion of galaxy by non humanoid aliens 20,000 year struggle for dominance

Empire crumbling – period of wars and isolation –
300,000 AD empire in many different hands

The 'Billion Ships' take man to the nearest galaxy – none return 200,000 AD Period (approx) of Foundation and importance of Trantor

100,000 AD Rise of first Galactic Empire

Hyperjump
eloped over 3,000 years
AD 1 Explosive colonization of galaxy by faster than light ships

Major glaciation 100,000 BC Cro-Magnon man

Neanderthal man

200,000 BC

Major glaciation
300,000 BC

400,000 BC

Major glaciation
500,000 BC Homo erectus – Peking man – fire in use

600,000 BC

Major glaciation 700,000 BC

800,000 BC

900,000 BC

Major glaciation Simple stone tools –
Australopithecine
1 Million BC man forms

12 THOUSAND BC – 10 THOUSAND AD

10,000 AD Stage set for explosive expansion of man into the galaxy

Colonization of many worlds including Pern and Mesklin

Outward expansion on small scale to nearby stars

Begin-again-day – man journeys to the moon

5,000 AD Technology maintained but not developed Man turns inwards and forgets the stars

Hypothetical end of universe

Generation ships in common use

Discovery of Ringworld
Discovery of Rama
Man lands on the moon

Man meets Puppeteers
First Okie Cities

Discovery of America by Europeans
Norman conquest of England

Fall of Rome AD 1 Arthur of the Britons
Christ on Earth

Rise of Roman empire

Iron in common use Solomon – Confucius – Assyrian empire

Stonehenge begun Great Pyramids – use of bronze – use of alphabet

Mycenaean civilization – Moses

Writing invented – use of copper – late Stone Age in western Europe (megaliths)

The wheel in common use

5,000 BC

New Stone Age – domestication of animals – formation of village life – worship of mother goddess

First farmers

Late hunting cultures – middle Stone Age and cave painting culture coming
Man's nomadic life ending – ice nearly gone
10,000 BC to an end

doing so) is to take some extreme aspect of conditions on Earth and extrapolate it to fill an entire planet. It is then possible for the imaginative author to create in detail a society designed to fit those special conditions without the ameliorative factor of an easier climate beyond the mountains or across the sea. Examples include – among many others – Gethen, in Ursula Le Guin's *The Left Hand of Darkness*, and the Blue World in Jack Vance's novel of the same name. In Le Guin's book we have a world of perpetual winter, with widespread Antarctic conditions (the accounts of the polar explorers are an acknowledged influence). But the novel is far more than an adventure in harsh terrain: Le Guin produces a complex and moving story to set against her wintry backdrop. Further, it gives her the opportunity to thrust together her two main characters in conditions of isolation and hardship, as they are forced to embark upon a long trek – an episode central and vital to the novel. Thus setting and story mesh: the form of the story is shaped by its setting, and draws its peculiar strengths from it.

Vance's novel introduces a planet *entirely* covered by ocean; its inhabitants, the People of the Floats – survivors of a crashed spaceship – lead easygoing lives on clusters of giant lilypads. More attention is paid to the scenery here – devising odd and colourful worlds and societies is Vance's forte – but the story is a quirky and enjoyable reworking of Jack the Giant-Killer, full of industrial revolution whose details are satisfyingly ingenious. (How *do* you set about refining metals on a planet where the only 'land' is a vegetable mass, with no ores to be mined?)

But the supreme example of this sort of planet-building is surely Frank Herbert's Arrakis, setting of the *Dune* trilogy. This is a world of deep desert, with extremes of desiccation impossible on a planet with substantial areas of free water. Indeed, water is poisonous to the major local lifeform, the giant sandworm. Herbert's native society is shaped, entirely and necessarily, by the extreme harshness of conditions, with survival dependent on constant attention to the need for water. The people's social customs and way of life are shaped by this overriding imperative; even the language Herbert gives them reflects their world with convincing ingenuity (e.g. in the numerous differing terms they have for what in our language is a single short word – 'sand'). The result is a world which seems convincingly *lived-in*, as real to the reader as it apparently is to the characters. This must be an important factor in the phenomenal success of the series.

Scientists' worlds One of the traditional pleasures of the 'hardcore' science fiction writer is designing objects which *work*, or at least give a convincing appearance of doing so. Such a writer, faced with the need to create an alien planet, will do so from the ground up. He will decide on the size and type of star, fix on likely orbits for its planets, allocate elements to his chosen world in plausible proportions and design a workable atmosphere and climate. He will then introduce a possible biosphere. For such a writer the initial creative act is likely to be performed with the aid of calculator, graph and tables – and clearly, only a writer who is also a trained scientist is likely to be able to perform the exercise. Some writers – Poul Anderson is an example – will do this homework as a matter of course, even if the world does not figure prominently in the story they intend to write. The argument is that the writer should be familiar with all this data even if he does not intend to make explicit use of it.

By common consent the master of scientific world-building is Hal Clement. Ingenious alien creations figure in such novels as *Cycle of Fire* and *Close to Critical,* but his greatest achievement is undoubtedly the weird planet Mesklin, perhaps the strangest invented world in science fiction. Reading of an aberration in the orbits of the two stars of the 61 Cygni B system, Clement deduced the possible existence of a large, rapidly spinning planet as a third member of the system. He then proceeded to design the world, taking account of the important geophysical and geochemical factors, and worked out a possible form of intelligent life. The discus-shaped planet, its gravitational attraction at the poles hundreds of times greater than that at the rim, suggested a narrative problem which would set his characters in motion to explore their world and open it up to the eye of the reader. It is a supreme example of imaginative creation.

Worlds which Grow Sometimes authors will create a world for the purpose of a story, and then find themselves returning to it again and again as the idea yields more possibilities than, perhaps, they had originally seen. Anne McCaffrey's Pern appears to be such a place. The original idea was to work out a rationale which would make possible the existence of fire-breathing dragons as real creatures rather than myths. The factors which make this plausible – the production of phosphine gas in their stomachs, and the invasive fungoid Threads which they use the fire to combat – followed ingeniously, but the first stories, amalgamated into the novel *Dragonflight,* were romantic adventures in which the background, both physical and social, was painted in broad strokes. As the series progressed the world was fleshed out in increasing detail, becoming more solid all the time – for example the complex structure of the

Craft Holds, and especially the musical crafts. Now, after five books, it is as real and solid an entity as any other invented world. This is creation from the top down, as it were, rather than the bottom up, with the author exploring and learning about her creation right alongside her characters. It is the precise opposite of the Hal Clement approach.

A similar example is Marion Zimmer Bradley's Darkover series, which started off as exotic science fantasy adventure, but which in recent novels has developed far greater complexity, enabling the author to write novels (as opposed to adventure stories) in its setting.

Artificial Worlds If an author can sit down and design and build a world from scratch, then why not postulate an advanced civilization who can do precisely the same . . . and then go out and build the thing? Such constructions are increasingly common in modern sf, following on the growth of interest in such ideas among speculative scientists. For instance, Freeman Dyson proposed that in order to maximize the use of its sun's energy, a technologically advanced race lacking means of interstellar travel would be well advised to break up its outer planets and use the pieces to form a shell about their solar system. In the process they would acquire enough living space to satisfy even the most fecund species for a very long time. He did not actually mean a *solid* shell – that would be an engineering impossibility – but rather a loose swarm of objects. However, this detail did not prevent science fiction writers from coming up with artificial planets based on the Dyson Sphere – Larry Niven's *Ringworld* and Bob Shaw's *Orbitsville*. Of the two, Niven is more concerned with the physical details of his creation (which is not an entire sphere but, as its name suggests, a thin slice – still a million miles across! – through one).

Similarly, proposals have been made for space colonies or space arks (the latter, essentially, being a mobile version of the former). These would be entire self-contained worlds, either remaining in solar orbit or embarking upon generations-long journeys to the stars (during which, in the classic sf treatments such as Heinlein's *Orphans of the Sky* and Aldiss's *Nonstop*, there is a reversion to savagery and the purpose of the journey – or even the fact that the inhabitants are on a journey – is forgotten). The preferred design is for a hollowed-out asteroid, or artificial cylinder or torus, rotated to provide artificial gravity. Inside is a deceptively natural-looking world, until you notice that the horizon curves upwards, and there are trees and buildings hanging vertically down from the 'ceiling' . . . While scientists like Gerard O'Neill of Princeton University and groups like the L-5 Society urge the building of the first real space colony, science fiction writers explore the ideas in novels like *Captive Universe* and *Rendezvous with Rama*. But no artificial world is more grandiose in conception than the flying cities of James Blish's 'Okie' series.

Alien Earth Of course it is possible to produce an alien landscape without ever leaving home. All you have to do is change the Earth. It's a process which has its dangers: nothing dates so fast as outdated views of the future, as witness many of the visions embalmed on the covers of old pulp magazines. Somehow a vista of a fantastic futuristic city seems far *more* than forty or fifty years old when you spot that propeller-driven biplane flitting across the foreground.

Natural or man-made disaster can accomplish radical changes, as shown in J.G. Ballard's trio of novels *The Drowned World*, *The Drought* and *The Crystal World*, where the Earth is altered in ways made obvious by the novels' titles. Another way is to let time take its course. Few worlds could be stranger than the distant future Earth of Aldiss's *Hothouse*, where the Moon has become stationary relative to the Earth and giant spiders spin their webs from one to another; few could be more broodingly effective than the vision of a dying world described in H.G. Wells's *The Time Machine* — perhaps the first true modern sf classic. On the vast timescales adopted by such books (or by others such as William Hope Hodgson's *The Night Land* or Olaf Stapledon's *Last and First Men*) human history as we know it becomes no more than a brief flicker in the immensities of time.

* * * *

There is a central debate in science fiction, which from time to time manifests itself under misleading labels such as 'hardcore' versus 'softcore' or 'old wave' versus 'new wave'. It has to do with the differing attractions of scientific realism and imaginative freedom. We have explored the way in which certain authors build up their invented landscapes in precise scientific detail. Other authors might suggest that the nature of an imaginary world is chosen to fit the purpose it is to serve, as setting or symbol, and that it does not matter in the least, as long as it is not jarring within the context of the story, whether or not that creation is scientifically defensible. The argument against that, from the scientifically-minded critic, may be that such impossibilities are *always* jarring – but that is a specialized objection from a specialized section of the audience. Such criticisms have been levelled at *Hothouse,* and they are technically valid: it *is* impossible to have spiders spinning their webs from the Earth to the Moon. The fact remains, though, that it was that particular imaginative vision which sparked off the whole novel – which no reader supposes to be a blueprint of future history – and it is essential to the book.

It is not possible to deal with invented worlds purely on a straightforward physical basis (although it may be fun to pretend, as in the text of this book, that they do all exist). Many of them also have deep roots in human psychology. One can see this in certain repeated motifs. Take the arid landscape of sand, rock and erosion, which has attracted talents as diverse as Salvador Dali, T.S. Eliot and J.G. Ballard. Such a setting evokes and reflects feelings of desolation and emptiness; of psychological aridity. This also infuses a setting like Arrakis; no matter how precisely worked out its physical detail, the associations remain.

Another example is the ruined world. We see this on Trantor, in the later stages of Isaac Asimov's *Foundation* trilogy: the ultimate in human technology – a planet which is one enormous city – falling into death and decay. We see (as in tales of the distant future) man's impotence in the face of the great forces of time and entropy. A world falling into ruin provides a perfect external reflection for feelings of loss or grief. See, for example, George R. R. Martin's *Dying of the Light,* where the dying world of Worlorn (whose name hints at sadness with its echo of 'forlorn') complements and strengthens a story of lost hopes and loves.

But however an alien landscape is brought into being – whether by careful calculation and speculation, where the author needs to be expert in astrophysics, chemistry, geology, biology, linguistics and much else besides, or by an act of unfettered imaginative creation – one thing is beyond doubt. There are few things in science fiction more satisfying to reader and writer alike than an alien landscape – real or artificial, on a future Earth or far across the galaxy – skilfully and convincingly brought to life.

Acknowledgements

This book would not have been possible without the imaginative efforts of the authors whose creations are featured in its pages. Our thanks and respect go to all of them. If you have read the books from which these landscapes are derived we hope you will enjoy the interpretation given here. If you have not read the books, we hope you will want to do so at the earliest opportunity.

They are as follows:

Rama	Rendezvous with Rama, by Arthur C. Clarke	**Arrakis**	Dune Dune Messiah Children of Dune, by Frank Herbert
Pern	Dragonflight Dragonquest Dragonsinger Dragonsong The White Dragon, by Anne McCaffrey	**Ringworld**	Ringworld, by Larry Niven
		Trantor	Foundation Foundation and Empire Second Foundation, by Isaac Asimov
Okie Cities	They Shall Have Stars A Life for the Stars Earthman, Come Home A Clash of Cymbals, by James Blish	**Hothouse**	Hothouse, by Brian Aldiss
Mesklin	Mission of Gravity Star Light, by Hal Clement	**End of the World**	The Time Machine, by H.G. Wells
Eros	Captive Universe, by Harry Harrison		

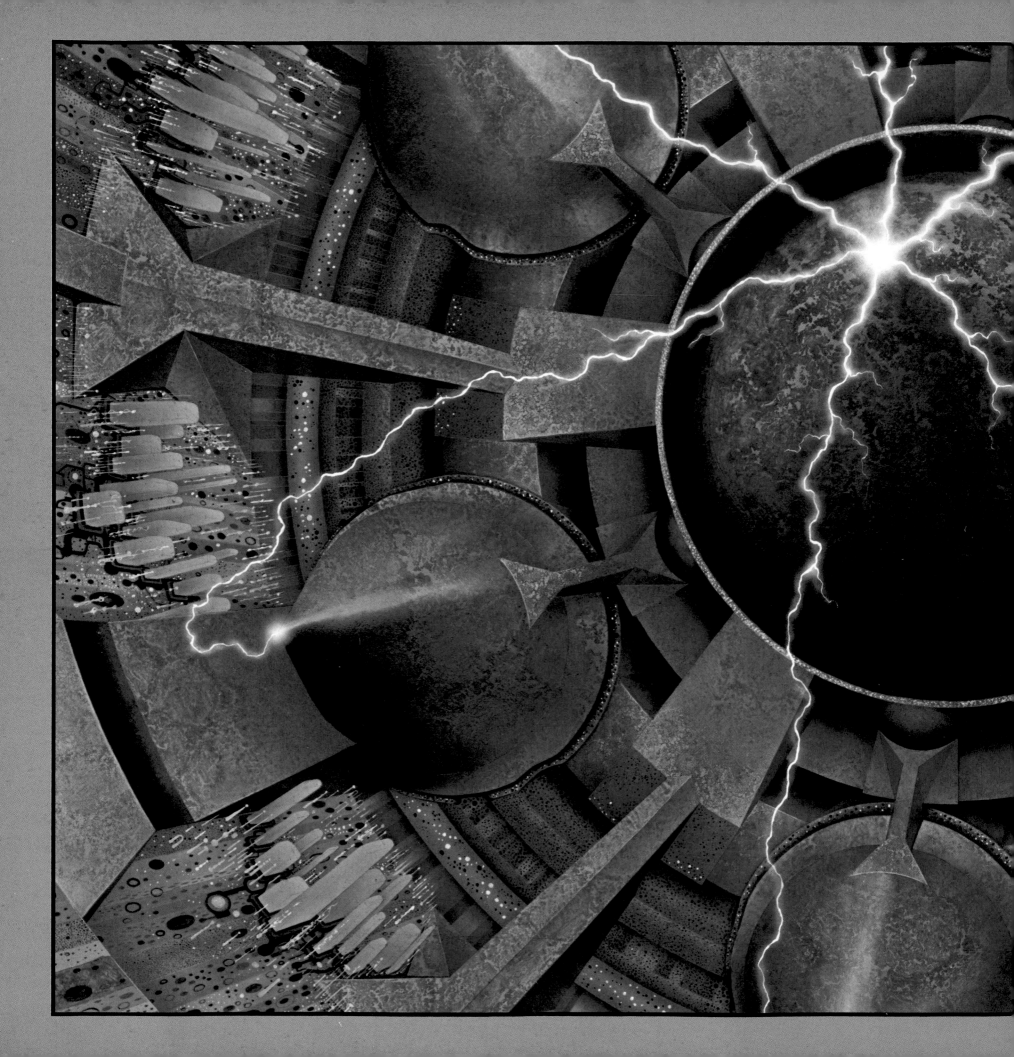

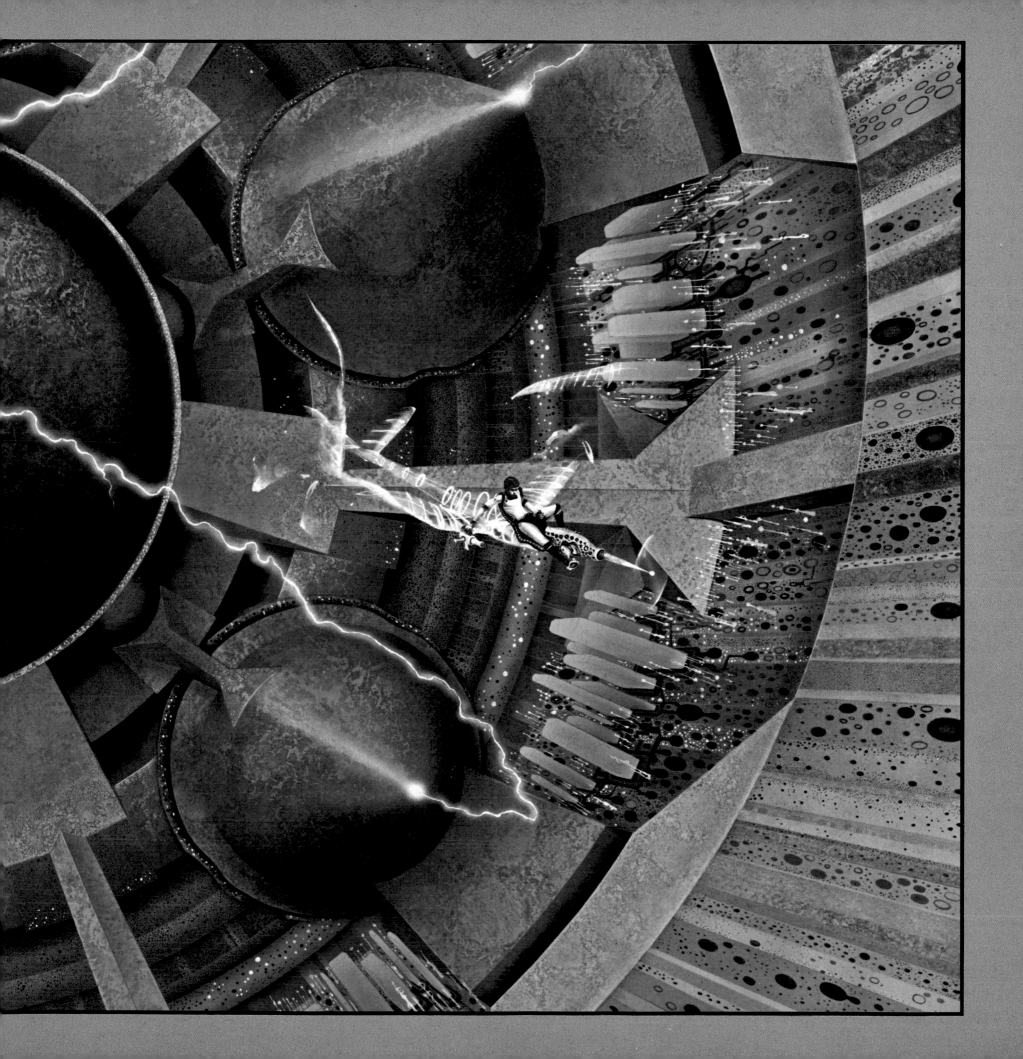

Rama

Mankind's first meeting with alien intelligence remains his most mysterious. The giant starship known as *Rama* passed through the solar system in the year 2130 (old dating system), allowing only a brief period of exploration. The results raised many more questions but provided few answers. To this day we do not know where *Rama* came from, where it was headed, why it visited the solar system, or who its builders were. Perhaps its visit was merely a refuelling stage, one of many on its long journey. We know that as it prepared to leave our solar system it came within five million kilometres of the sun, having first produced a highly reflective shield to avert the danger of melting at such close proximity to the immense heat. As it passed it appeared to absorb not only the energy but the actual matter of the sun itself! *Rama's* journey must be one of the longest ever undertaken. Projections of its inward trajectory showed that it was more than 200,000 years since it previously passed near a sun – and that one was an irregular variable star which could not possibly have been its point of origin. Even now it is somewhere out in the depths of interstellar space, its systems shut down, waiting through the millennia until the warmth of some other star brings it briefly back to life…

The physical details of *Rama* are straightforward and impressive enough. The spaceship was a cylinder, externally featureless save for three pillbox-shaped structures at the end where the airlocks were found. It was fifty kilometres in length and twenty in diameter. The hull was about half a kilometre thick (though what it contained we do not know). The total mass was in the region of ten thousand billion tons. The ship rotated about its axis to produce artificial gravity in the hollow interior.

Within the cylinder, at the end where the airlocks were, three massive stairways led down to the 'ground'. (Trilateral symmetry was characteristic of everything on *Rama*.) This was named the North End of the ship. At the other extremity, the South End, there was no such arrangement. In the centre an immense spike extended five kilometres into the interior. Around it six smaller spikes, two and a half kilometres in length, were arrayed symmetrically. Their function remains a mystery, although they were responsible for spectacular electrical discharges which accompanied the storms that built up inside the ship as it grew warmer on its approach to the sun. Illumination was provided by six immense striplights which ran the length of the ship, interrupted only by its most spectacular geographical feature, the Cylindrical Sea.

Imagine sailing on a sea where the east and west horizons curve away upwards, eventually meeting directly above your head. That was the disorienting prospect which confronted the intrepid explorers of *Rama*. But it was a sea with differences.

Firstly, it was liable to generate immense tidal waves as the ship manoeuvred, and was thus equipped with anti-slosh plates which quickly damped down any large waves that formed. Secondly, it fulfilled a vital role in providing a home for billions of micro-organisms as *Rama*, bringing itself back to life, recapitulated the processes of millions of years of evolution in a matter of days (see below).

This much general description is all that is possible. We can also look (albeit with more wonder than understanding) at certain of its striking features:

New York Dotted about *Rama's* surface were a number of mysterious structures which the explorers named for terrestrial cities. New York was the most interesting of these, situated as it was in the middle of the Cylindrical Sea. It had three identical structures, built on an oval base. Each of these structures was itself divided into three, which meant the 'city' consisted of nine identical elements, each of which soared hundreds of metres into the sky. It appeared to be a gigantic machine, perhaps involved in the production of biots (see below), but it was not observed functioning.

Biots The word is a contraction of 'biological robots', the term used to describe the curious machines-cum-lifeforms which appeared during *Rama's* transit. When the spaceship first approached the solar system it was assumed that it must be completely dead. It had, after all, been travelling for a minimum of 200,000 years, and even the most sophisticated techniques of suspended animation or cryogenic freezing permit irreversible cell damage after a matter of centuries. No one thought, until it happened, that *Rama* might be programmed to create life when conditions permitted. The first sign was the sudden proliferation of organisms in the Cylindrical Sea. These produced oxygen which regenerated the ship's atmosphere. Then a variety of creatures appeared, to baffle the explorers as they exhibited some characteristics of machinery and others of organic life.

One of the most common forms was the Scavenger. This was a crablike creature some two metres long. It was equipped with claws which it used to cut up any useful items of debris it found. Manipulative organs like human hands then deposited the pieces on to its back to be dumped for recycling into the Sea or into one of three pits in the southern hemisphere (or hemicylinder) of *Rama*. In its mouth area it had what appeared to be a selection of tools, and its shell appeared to be polished metal. A second species was the Spider. This was essentially a mobile sensory device, consisting of a body with three equally-spaced eyes on top of a tripod. It moved with a curious whirling action, using each leg in turn as a pivot. A fortuitous accident to a Spider enabled the explorers to carry out a dissection. It showed that the creature was organic, although it lacked any respiratory, digestive or reproductive system. It had quite a complex brain, but 80% of its body consisted of electric cells, like those used by certain terrestrial animals as a means of defence. To the Spider they were a source of energy: it seemed to be no more or less than an electric-powered reconnaissance device, alive but clearly designed to perform a specific task.

Many other species of biots were observed: the Sharks, which sliced up any useful material that found its way into the Cylindrical Sea; the Window Cleaners, which used their padded feet to polish the glassy surface material of *Rama's* lights; the mobile cranes like two-headed giraffes. But no other opportunity for close inspection presented itself.

Temple of Glass The explorers only cut their way into one of the sealed, featureless buildings which they found. Inside there were hundreds of regularly-spaced crystalline columns about a metre in diameter. Each column contained a hologram, visible only from certain angles. The arrangement of holograms appeared entirely random: peculiar hand tools, domestic utensils, scientific instruments, and scores of unidentifiable objects were jumbled together. It was theorized that the building might be a catalogue of Raman objects, throwing up odd juxtapositions in just the same way as an alphabetical dictionary. Unfortunately the exploration was curtailed as *Rama's* systems began to shut down preparatory to its passage near the sun, but not before the only clue was found to the nature of the Ramans.

The Ramans No intelligent being was found aboard *Rama*; nor was any photograph or hologram. But the Temple of Glass did yield an image of what was evidently a Raman uniform, and it is on this that all theoretical reconstructions are based. The creature appeared to be some two and a half metres in height, not counting its head (assuming it had one). The waist was very narrow; the 'shoulder' area was broad – about a metre in diameter – and there were apparently three arms and three legs. Such an arrangement might have been predicted from the design of the Spiders and from the pervasive emphasis on trilateral symmetry on *Rama*.

The Cylindrical Sea *(overleaf)*
The human explorers of *Rama* investigated the Cylindrical Sea on a raft cleverly improvised from empty storage drums. Here, with the complex structures of 'New York' filling the middle distance, we see them surprised by the sudden appearance of one of the largest biots encountered on *Rama*. The starfish-like creature broke the surface after being crippled by one of the tidal waves which swept the Cylindrical Sea, and was subsequently demolished by other biots. Overhead, in *Rama's* 'sky', can be seen the immense striplights which illuminated the huge ship's interior.

The main result of *Rama's* passage was to open irreversibly humanity's eyes to the knowledge that they were not alone in the Universe. Of course there were upheavals: a millenarian religious revival, an outbreak of savage (but shortlived) xenophobia, a rash of books claiming to prove from archaeological evidence that Ramans had visited Earth in prehistoric times. (There was some justification for considering this seriously. As the Ramans appeared to do everything by threes some scientists conjectured that two further spaceships might be expected. Equally, however, *Rama* might have been the second or third ship, with the others having arrived centuries before). One of the most trivial by-products, though, is the one by which *Rama* is best remembered today: the variety of highly-detailed children's models and construction kits which are now expensive and sought-after collectors' items. Popular reproductions of these antiques help to keep alive the memory of the greatest mystery from our past.

Pern

Pern An earth-type world circling the yellow (G-type) star Rukbat, located in the Sagittarian Sector of the Galaxy. Third planet from the sun of five, exclusive of two belts of asteroidal material (probably disintegrated worlds) Pern's main colonized continent (the northern) was dramatically mountainous, with sprawling fertile river plains between, especially close to *Crom*, *Telgar*, *Igan* and *Keroon* regions (all bordered by deep foothills). The Southern Continent proved too inhospitable for successful existence. Economic dependence of *Holds* & *Weyrs* (see below) in High Reaches and other mountain regions was acute and Pernese economy was complex and based on principles of co-operative interdependence (see *Crafts*). Rukbat was unusual in that it had captured a stray planet during the few thousand years prior to man's colonization of Pern. The stranger, visualized as a moving red star, orbited Rukbat in an elliptical path, quite different from natural sibling worlds. Although it was lost from the mainstream of galactic development during the period of consolidation and suffered survival difficulties following the first attack by the 'red star' and the indigenous life form that inhabited it, it is known that Pern was the location of one of the most dramatic and astonishing man-alien symbioses, a telepathic and co-operative relationship with the 'dragon' forms that had evolved there.

Pern Dragons So-called after the terrestrial mythical beasts supposed to have been fire-breathing, winged, reptilian anachronisms (and a term often applied to the successful limbless Earth reptile family of snakes) the Dragons of Pern were intelligent creatures with a highly developed empathic communication capability. They were gentle animals, often growing to gigantic size, with long narrow necks and triangular wedge-shaped heads. With their large and highly functional wings, Pern dragons were adept at flying, though less comfortable during ground motion. The fire-breathing is thought to have been a highly specialized adaptation to the threat of alien invasion (see *Threads*): the fire came from lumps of phosphine-bearing rock, *firestone*, eaten by the dragons and held in the cavernous stomachs until emitted as a flaming gas. One other feature of the dragons which is of special interest is their teleportation ability, referred to as going *between*. It is a psychic power capable of transferring dragon and rider not only across pan-planetary distances in a single instant, but also between times (although the full capability of the time-element of the power is not known). Several morphological forms of dragons are known, basically distinguished by colour, size, growth rate, fighting ability and empathic capability. Body colours of blue, green and

Mating ritual *(overleaf)*
Above one of the more natural-looking Holds on the planet Pern, the mating of the Queen occurs 'on the wing'. Dragons of all colours fly around, resting now that they have lost the battle for the Queen's affection. The successful bronze dragon entwines its body about the beautiful golden Queen and fertilizes the eggs she carries. On the ground, in the vast arena edged by caves and fire-ridges, the human colonists watch both the sky-mating of the telepathic, native life-forms, and the possession of the Queen's rider, the Weyr-woman, by the rider of the bronze, the Weyr-leader himself. The girl, who has not yet ridden any dragon at all, shares the Queen's ecstasy, empathically linked with the alien. The fury of the contest still shows in the new Weyr-leader's face as he waits to possess the Weyr-woman in the human way.

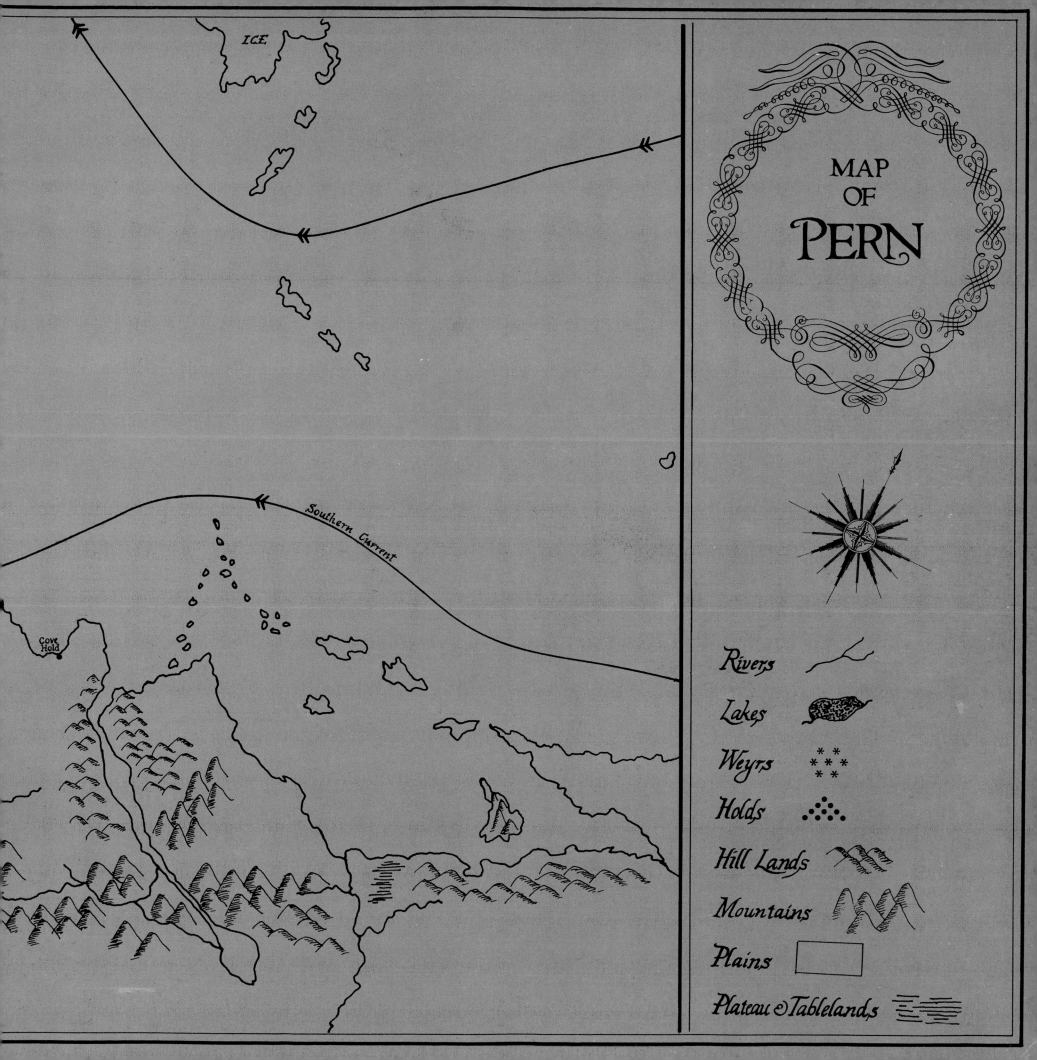

ICE

MAP
OF
PERN

Southern Current

Cove
Hold

Rivers

Lakes

Weyrs

Holds

Hill Lands

Mountains

Plains

Plateau & Tablelands

brown, are known, but the most important dragon forms were the bronzes, the most powerful and competitively superior (and always wing-leaders), and the golden Queen, whose ritual mating occurred above the great Weyr, and whose hatch was the sole genesis of more dragons.

Threads Invasive life-forms, originating from the 'red star' or captured planetary body of Rukbat. Mycorrhizoid-spore forms, the Threads were capable of escaping their own planetary gravity and traversing the 'warm' space of the Rukbat solar reaches, penetrating Pern's atmosphere and descending to the earth as long, highly fertile and fecund, and highly deadly 'threads'. Invasion occurred only at closest approach of two worlds, thus accounting for long delays (generations) between attacks. The nature of the invasive process, whether intelligence based or a bizarre adaptation to hostile planetary environment, is obscure. The fire-breathing capability of Pernese dragons enables most atmospheric penetrations to be countered, although there is evidence that some such encounters have not been entirely successful.

Weyrs The original settlements of the first 'dragon folk', the terran descendants who were in symbiosis with the native life-form. They were vast stone and wooden constructions in and around the cave-pocked slopes of the six vast extinct volcanoes on the continent. Here both man and dragon shared an existence, watching across the lowlands for the invasive Threads, and supported, due to the non-productivity of their surroundings, by the rest of the scattered population. The smaller, more common human habitation, the *Hold*, was built wherever the terrain afforded protection or strategic emplacement, mostly in and on cave-ridden cliffs. They rose majestically above the land as cold, dark havens of humankind; for example, *Ruatha Hold*. The caves were made more accessible to each other by fashioning ridges out of rock face; the communities were lit by fire-ridges, lines of fire spreading across the face. At first these caves were havens of man and dragon, but as the dragons grew large so the rock-walled Holds were built on top of the cave cliffs . . . and so watch towers, buildings and arenas sprung up.

Crafts Pernese society was highly ordered and disciplined, and the Craft Hall of each Hold was of major importance. Crafts were many and varied; weaving, metal and wood working, farming and fishing, and instrument making. Each craft looked towards one

Master Craft Hall, not necessarily in the same Hold or Weyr. The Master Craft Hall trained craftsman, and co-ordinated the distribution of craft products. Craft halls were outside the jurisdiction of the Hold and the Lord Holder, in order to equalize the benefit of their skills and productions across the whole planet. Music was important to Pern society, with musicians being regarded very highly, in particular the Harpers; instruments ranged from the large Harp, the lap Harp, to weyr-skin drums, pipes and stringed, strumming instruments called *gitars,* modified from the classic terran instrument.

Weyr-riders & Weyr-women Dragon riders and guardians against the Threads. Weyr-riders ride the bronze, blue, green and brown dragons, whereas the Weyr-women, one per Weyr, are riders of the golden Queen dragon. The relationship is very special between Queen and Weyr-woman, and between Weyr-woman and Weyr-leader, the rider of the bronze that successfully mates with the Queen.

(from Dunn's Cosmic Gazetteer, 17th ed.)

Ruatha Hold *(overleaf)*
High on the valley slopes, between Crom and Fort Weyr in the south, the medieval walls of Ruatha Hold bear stark witness to the early struggles of mankind to find a footing on the planet Pern. Stone walls, iron gates and the deep caves where the original settlers found shelter from the elements, now house a highly independent and sensitive people, who live in harmony with the land and with the dragons of the nearby Weyr. High above this deep valley a dragon can be seen entering the warm world again from the icy cold of *between,* a non-space region into which both dragon and rider can fly, using the dragon's strange, ancient powers of mind. *Between* can take them to all places and all times.

Okie Cities

Suggested Reading

*Hands Across the Galaxy: a review of the
formation of the Astral League: vol 1, the
Okies*, compiled and edited by Professor
Donald West (University of Trantor
Press, N.U.E. 26597)

What was the connection between a frantic laboratory search for some way to see Rotifer chromosomes, back in the late 20th century, and the remote controlled construction of a bridge made out of Ice IV, and built as near to the surface of Jupiter as man could get? And how did these apparently unconnected events, plus a spinning Uni-pole, give rise to man's first major effort to bridge the immense void between our Galaxy and the Lesser Magellanic Clouds? The answers are part of the technological evolution of early man, and the almost ironic way in which connections can fail to be noticed until the time is right. If every step of human progress, reaching back to the pre-Industrial age, had been instantly assessed in all its relationships with other areas of progress, it is quite likely that the fall of the West would not have occurred in *circa* 2105. Man would long since have found himself in control of the Macrocosm of the Universe, and the microcosm of his own society and mentality. The history of man's expansion into the Galaxy is one of opportunities created, as each phase in his technological evolution was reached and absorbed. The remote controlled manipulation of vast masses of ice, and the information it made available concerning gravity and the relationship between *mass* and *spin*, eventually led to the first flying cities leaving the star shores of the Milky Way and crossing the void of intergalactic space; the anti-agathic drugs delayed ageing without affecting mental function and made such journeys possible for the human inhabitants of those 'Okies', the Cities in Flight.

Cities in Flight – the words conjure a magic vision of enormous hemispherical structures sailing serenely between the worlds. There isn't a child on any planet of the Galaxy that doesn't own a SpacToy 'Spinnie', or who hasn't made a one-ten-thousandth replica working model of New York. There are over 4000 different versions, different toy types, based on the old Okie star-travel. Kids love them – they represent a part of the old technology, of the beginnings of a conquest now so long lost. And they represent something else: they represent man at his most successful – because the Flying Cities *worked*. They were efficient, they were practical, they were the best thing that happened to Aspiring Man, the early men who set their sights on the stars.

The question is, just how much of our respect and love for the Okies is for real? Just how much of that aspiration and achievement do we *really* remember, all these thousands of years after it all happened? Let me ask you a question. How many Okie cities were built on asteroids and sent out into the void? A hundred? A thousand? Ten thousand? OK, so you don't know. Let's try another one. How many flying cities were modelled after New York? Remember New York from history? A city on Earth, on the East coast of America. So what's the answer? How many flying cities? I haven't caught you out, I can tell. Just one, right? Wrong!

No Okie Cities *at all* were modelled after New York. The Okie city of New York *was* New York – for real! The actual, living city, every last bit of concrete, steel, glass, every road, every office, every coffee shop, every dustbin, every drunk and disorderly, every paving stone – the whole city of New York was lifted *bodily* and flung out into space. It's probably still there, somewhere, out between the Galaxies.

What made all this possible was the 'spindizzy'. Remember that Bridge on Jupiter? All that work on spin and mass and gravity? The spindizzy grew directly out of that work – an antigravity machine that was more than an antigravity machine, because it also threw up a protective field that kept warmth and air in, and space and cold out.

There's a book by a man called Acreff-Monales. It's called *The Milky Way, Five Cultural Portraits*, and you can get it in any good library, or any microstore information system. Somewhere in that book he has this to say:*

Once antigravity was an engineering reality, it was no longer necessary to design ships for space travel, for neither mass nor aerodynamic lines meant anything any more. The most massive and awkward object could be lifted and hurled off the Earth, and carried almost any distance. Whole cities, if necessary, could be moved.

It's all there in 'copAlloy' circuits, down in the holo-chips . . . even in black and white. But we've forgotten it, we've changed our beliefs. Why I wonder? Don't forget that all this happened before the hyperjump, before the Galaxies became measurable not in light years, but in J numbers. And the generation ships had been going out for years, secretly more often than not, and none of them using any really practical systems of survival. They used either generations breeding as on Earth, or thousands of populace stuck in suspended animation. The Flying Cities took advantage of immortality drugs! They killed the generation ship . . . but they couldn't kill the boredom of endless space travel, even though ships and cities could now travel faster than the speed of light.

What we've done is to forget the reality in its fine detail, instead remembering a *romantic* idea . . . the space-techs and builders constructing hugh cities on asteroids, and pushing them starwards on massive antigravity engines. As if the reality of lifting whole cities off the Earth wasn't startling enough! But somehow it's not as romantic, right? So we mix the two things together, and get something that's half right, and a

*quoted in the novel *Earthmen, Come Home*, by James Blish

Okie City, lift-off *(overleaf)*
The first cities to wrench themselves out of the rock and soil of the Earth, were the industrial cities of the American Continent; this picture, showing the preparation for flight of the city of Scranton, vividly captures the drama and upheaval of those first few moments. The city rocks on its horizontal axis, dust and rock falling from the edges of the crust where the spindizzy field has severed the city's connection with its parent planet. The inhabitants are protected from the gravitational pull of the Earth by those same spindizzy motors whose field has now become their atmosphere, their space-ship hull. The city spins for a while, turning in the crater it has left behind it, before rising serenely and sailing out into the dark of space.

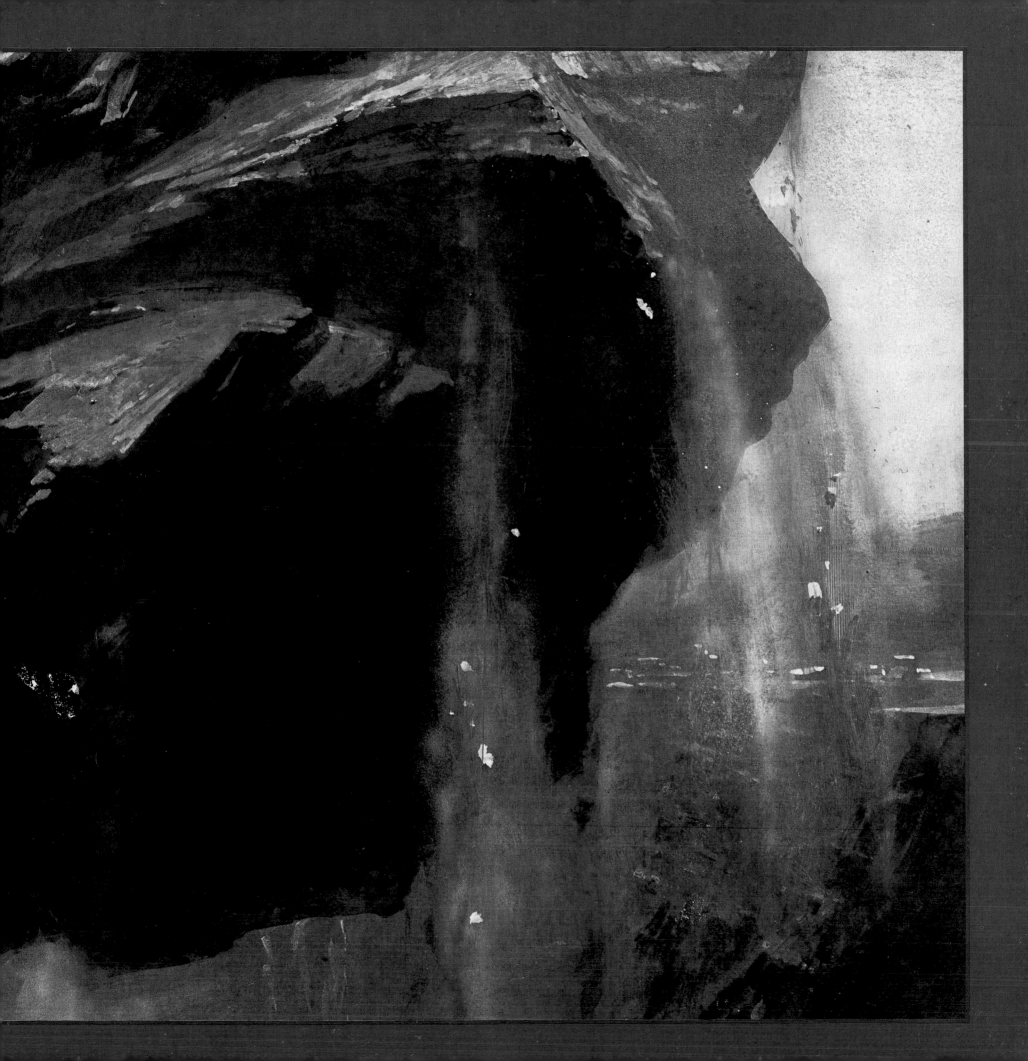

Okie City, trading contact (*previous page*)
In orbit around a colonized world, the Okie
City of New York, with its familiar Manhattan
Skyline, makes contact with a space vessel
sent up by the colonists to make first trade-
contact. Such stops frequently include the
transfer of personnel, some city dwellers
deciding to apply for immigration
permission, some colonists requesting
permission to come aboard the flying city
and make a life for the stars.

whole lot wrong. And of course, once New York had been blasted off Earth, out of the Solar System and into space on its dizzy wings, a new New York was built back on the Home World. It's still there, and it's easy to understand how it has come to be considered the original.

There's another book, by a man called James Blish, written about the time the Cities were leaving Earth.* It describes a city preparing to rise, and just listen to this for description and weep over the Compu-Gen Fiction the machine writers of today give us:

The whole city seemed to be rocking heavily, like a ship in a storm. At one instant the street ended in nothing but sky; at the next Chris was staring at a wall of sheared earth, its rim looming cliff-like, fifty feet or more above the new margin of the city; and then the blank sky was back again . . . Now the city was level again, amidst an immense cloud of dust through which Chris could see the landscape begin to move solemnly past him. The city had stopped rocking and was now turning slowly . . .

That description is of the take-off of the old city of Scranton, a mining, industrial city. There were hundreds such, and they were the first to take advantage of the new technology and lift their roots – and a considerable chunk of the planetary crust, incidentally – and drift like nomads about the world, sniffing out new resources. They mined and gutted and left whole lands wasted; they devastated Earth, and as if not content with that, when Earth became unprofitable they went into space. They gutted Mars and the Asteroids, and no doubt they took a good long, hard look at the other moons and worlds of the Solar System before they fled beyond Sol and became the Traders of the Stars, connecting colonized worlds in a much more acceptable way.

And that's why the Cities in Flight, despite their ultimate demise, were and are so important to you and me, because they initiated and carried on an age-old principle of peace, a principle that has to be re-learned with every frontier, and every new land. When you spread your people thinly, and widely, they lose contact. It's all very well knowing that over that hill, or on that world, there's another tribe just like you. The trouble is, unless you have trade you can't keep tabs on them. One day they've developed a better weapon than you, and then they've suddenly left you behind and you're not part of the same tribal system because you're not part of the same culture. So when you have traders you have contact and exchange of ideas and information . . . you have co-operation! The Okie cities brought co-operation to the early Galaxy, and

*A Life for the Stars

allowed colonial worlds to begin their lives as part of a system, and not as individuals. The traders suffered, though. Traders always do. You want to take out some anger, or frustration on someone, take it out on the traders, the contact men. So you can read all about how some cities were burned, and others not allowed landing permits on some worlds. But no matter what was happening to individual cities, the principle of contact was in force. The Galaxy was off to a good start, and we have the Okies to thank for the peace and prosperity of our own immense Universe today.

And all because a man in a laboratory was playing around with chemicals to show up the genetic molecules of a tiny fresh-water animal, and came up with a molecule that set the wheels in motion for an immortality drug, that we no longer use, but which meant that men could take to the stars without the fear of distances, even though they had the ability to travel at the speed of light and more, because a bridge builder on Jupiter had found the link between spin and mass and gravity, and had designed a machine which he called a 'spindizzy' that could affect antigravity, and protect everything within its field of play, a machine that we no longer use, because of the hyperjump. But without it, there would never have been a Galaxy worth jumping between.

(adapted from *Berk's Cosmic Links: the unexpected relationships between technology and some other things*, first shown on Solar State Holovid)

Burning City *(overleaf)*
As New York flies through the Great Rift, the starless void between the spiral arms of the Galaxy, it comes into contact with a burning Okie City. The City has been attacked and raided by a Dark City, a pirate, which drifts in the gloom and watches the result of its attack, wondering if New York will take punitive action against it. Such pirates are quite common, looting the traders for their immense wealth. New York, the biggest of the Okie Cities, is too large and too well defended to risk such an attack. The burning city is dead, its spindizzy field gone, its population instantly exposed to the cold of space. Its blackened, gutted hulk will float in the Great Rift forever.

Mesklin

Suggested Reading

1. *Conservation and non-interference motivations in Post-Industrial Space Exploration Programmes*, by J. T. Kirk (Enterprise Press, N.U.E. 24453)

2. *Strange Worlds and Creatures*, by Christopher P. Carlsen (Edwards Empire Building Pub., N.U.E. 26785)

3. *Legendary Worlds of the Galaxy: the fact and the fiction*, by Citizen H. C. Stubbs (TransGalactic ViewBooks, Boötes, N.U.E. 26955)

4. 'Whirligig World', by Hal Clement (first published in *Astounding Science Fiction*, June, Year 8 Atomic Era)

The planet Mesklin was discovered very early in the expansionist period of the human population, when planetary exploration was very much in its infancy. Few clues are available as to the location of this bizarre world, and little information survives, but from what is revealed in a number of very early sources it is quite apparent that Mesklin was an important world to the expanding human Empire, both because of its indigenous life-form (the Mesklinites) and because of the information this very high-gravity world could make available concerning the nature of gravity, and other physical laws. Modern feeling as to the location of Mesklin is mixed. Some sources suggest that it no longer exists, destroyed by the enormous forces inherent in its rotational velocity; however, in his neuroBook *Conservationist and non-Interference Motivations in post-Industrial Space Exploration Programmes*, Kirk suggests that the vital information needed to locate Mesklin among the peripheral star worlds was deliberately obliterated in order to protect the Mesklinites from the ravages of the First Empire[1]. The most likely location, however, is that suggested in Dunn's *Cosmic Gazetteer*, and based on the early work of Hal Clement, namely that Mesklin was the third 'heavy' body in the 61 Cygni double-star system: the smaller, and fainter, of the two orange suns in the binary pair did not move about the larger in a conventional elliptical path, but moved about Mesklin as part of a minor pair, which in turn moved about the major sun in the system. This proposal awaits verification.

Mesklin was an astonishing world, among the most bizarre of the 'natural' planets[2]. It was not a spheroid, the universal shape imposed on planetary objects condensing from gaseous stellar matter in the early stages of System formation – Mesklin in fact was *discus* shaped, narrower from pole to pole than it was across the equator. It seems certain that in *old miles* the dimensions of the world were 20,000 miles measured through the planet from one ammonia-snow covered pole to the other, and 48,000 miles measured from one 'rim' or equatorial edge to the other. A fat discus, then; a shape that requires some explanation as to how it could have evolved.

The answer is surely the immense rotational velocity of the world, coupled with its massive gravitational attraction – nearly 700 times Earth Normal (G) at the poles. As normal centrifugal forces pushed planetary material further from the spherical norm, the gravitational attraction of the massive core maintained the world in an intact state.

Rotating in the horizontal plane, then, lent to Mesklin exaggerated gravitational *and* climatic features. At the equatorial belt, which formed the rim of the world, the speed of rotation was so large that centrifugal forces played an enormous role in atmospheric disturbance. The gravity at the rim was about 3G, tolerable for a human explorer supported in an armoured suit; this gravity rose swiftly with approach to the poles and early explorers must have been effectively 'locked' into a narrow zone of the planet, by their available suit-technology.

It was the availability of the enormous polar gravity, and the highly variable gravitational field on Mesklin, that made it of interest to early space-researchers – very special equipment had to be designed to contain measuring instruments sent down to the polar regions, because if anything went wrong there would be no way, short of enlisting the help of the native life-form, of reaching that installation[3]. In fact, one such instance does come down to us in the literature, concerning the recovery of a polar probe by an expedition of Mesklinite traders, who took their raft and a metal sledge on a 45,000 mile trek on behalf of a small human operation. Clement's account of their journey, and the sub-species or 'varieties' of Mesklinite they encountered, remains one of the most vivid sources of description about Mesklin.

Mesklin was the planet of a double-star system, of which one was known locally either as *Esstes* or more familiarly 'the night sun'; a distant, dim, reddish star (K7), it was brighter than Earth's moon, but not bright enough to appear to be more than 'reflecting' light. The larger star, *Belne*, was the daytime sun, slightly hotter (K5) and much closer, a deep, brilliant golden colour. Because of Mesklin's rotational difference, towards the equatorial rim of the world Belne appeared to pass across the sky in 9 standard minutes. The Mesklinite traders had a notion of time unconnected with the passage of their 9 minute days since day length varied so extremely. Mesklin's two moons appear to have been large, undistinguished planetoids, orbiting at some distance from the World and used as human observation bases.

By all the evidence Mesklin was a world hostile not only gravitationally but meteorologically. Its atmosphere was largely hydrogen, and its seas not oceans of water, but oceans of liquid methane. A natural product of storm and evaporation was ammonia, which covered the poles as 'snow' and formed into towering clouds and vicious winds. The world, rotating so rapidly and warmed and cooled so erratically, was the site of incredible storms generated in much the same way as terrestrial hurricanes, by evaporation of the surface layers of oceans under the influence of sun. Unlike terrestrial storms, however, where water vapour rises above the denser atmosphere and contributes to the build up of the hurricane as it gives up heat on condensing, on Mesklin the evaporated methane was denser than the hydrogenous

Storm on Mesklin (*overleaf*)
A trader raft is swept towards an island-haven by one of Mesklin's furious equatorial storms. Mesklin, the bizarre discus-shaped world of 61 Cygnus, spins so fast on its axis that immense coriolis forces whip methane seas and ammonia clouds into hurricane-force cyclones. Formed in much the same way as terrestrial hurricanes, storms on Mesklin are self-limiting due to the lightness of the hydrogen atmosphere, which prevents 'rising currents'. Nevertheless, a storm at sea is something that Mesklinite traders always fear. Their rafts are flexible and tough – as indeed are the tiny Mesklinites themselves – but they know when to run and seek sheltered waters.

Storm debris on Mesklin *(previous page)*
A hurricane has raged across the equatorial area of Mesklin wreaking immense damage to life and land, and reaching deep into the sea itself. This huge deep-ocean creature has been cast onto a sandy beach, dead and rotting. An Earthman, wearing the heavy, limb-supporting suit that enables him to walk despite the 6 times normal gravity, tries to dig a sample of the creature for analysis, but he has no instrument strong enough to tear the 'teak-wood' like tissue of the monster. The tiny Mesklinites, a group of traders, gather round to watch, and solve the problem themselves; their forward pincers are able to cut tungsten steel, and they snip off pieces of the creature with ease, eating more than they give to the Earthman.

atmosphere and therefore rapidly limited the rising currents that were building up into a storm. Nonetheless, information from one source in particular suggests that storms on Mesklin were certainly fierce and not to be reckoned with lightly.[4]

The oceans, too, had distinct character. High tides at spring brought the sea-levels up to the Mesklinite cities themselves, but during the summer the ocean-level dropped, by evaporation, until by autumn those same cities were anything from two hundred to two thousand miles from the sea! The oceans were not colourless, but multi-coloured, a sign of the teeming microscopic – and often gigantic – life that lived in it.

Mesklin, in fact, was an abundantly populated world, in many ways quite primitive in that, for example, the oceanic carnivorous niche was occupied largely by creatures of enormous proportion, and in other ways quite exquisitely adapted to the particular geophysical and chemical conditions of the world – the tissue structure of motile life-forms, for example, was sufficiently strong to withstand the enormous gravitational pull of the world, and was structured so that it could withstand the varying gravity at different surface points. Flexibility, particularly of musculature, was inevitably a problem on Mesklin, a biological problem almost certainly resolved by 'compartmentalization' of tissue, or segmentation (see below). The predominant vegetative life form was a 'tree form', a soil binding, sheltering, nutrient-recycler. These were low, flat growths, with wide-spreading tentacular limbs and very short, thick trunks. In regions of low gravity their branches arched quite clear of the ground and intertwined to form a solid, dense, single growth layer.

And of course there were the Mesklinites themselves, intelligent creatures that are also recorded as having assisted in the exploration of the uninhabitable world of Dhrawn. The Mesklinites were a single species, but with an enormous range of varieties and cultures. There seem to have been populations living mostly inland who were at an advanced 'stone culture' level of development, and on isolated islands, by contrast, were varieties of the main life-stock that had a sophisticated comprehension of air technology, so much so that they were able to construct and launch gliders of simple, but highly efficient, design.

The conquest of the air by these 'hidden' populations suggests that there was a wide differentiation of psychological attitudes among the species. There is much evidence to suggest that Mesklinites, especially those living in high to extremely-high gravitational zones, were inordinately fearful of the concept of objects being raised above the ground. They would never contemplate hiding themselves *beneath* solid objects, even small ones, for if the object fell its weight would be crushing. Similarly the concept of actually 'throwing' an object seems to have been quite alien to many populations. With a falling velocity of many thousands of feet per second even an explosive-powered bullet would have hit the ground within a few inches from the muzzle of the gun. Most of these facts concerning Mesklinite behaviour come from the account of the trader-mission to the south pole. Most of the coastal-living populations seem to have specialized as traders, keeping the varieties in tenuous contact with each other, and sailing the methane seas on rafts constructed out of many tiny rafts sewn together, and moved by flimsy cloth sails. Unlike earth populations of the primitive era, there is no evidence that 'shuttle' culture, the spread of ideas outwards from narrow contact zones, occurred.

The Mesklinites were segmented creatures not unlike, in certain respects, terrestrial caterpillars. Most descriptions available refer to the coastal traders, who averaged in length up to eighteen inches. Inland there appear to have been 'giants', some up to three feet in length. They moved on dozens of legs, each leg ending with a wide sucker-like foot; they had several eyes, protected by thick, transparent eye-shields. The front third of the body could raise itself vertically and the first four pairs of legs were here modified into pincer-tipped arms of enormous strength (they could cut tungsten steel) and yet highly precise and delicate. Their body colour varied according to variety, but was mainly red and black.

Glider attack on Mesklin (*overleaf*)
Dusk is rapidly approaching as *Belne*, the nearer, brighter of Mesklin's suns, sinks rapidly towards the horizon. *Esstes*, distant and seen paler than usual through the gathering ammonia clouds, is not bright enough to be more than Mesklin's 'night sun'. A trader raft, forty small raft-units knitted together with rope, flees along a river of liquid methane, towards the distant mountains that border the sea. The gliders are unfamiliar to the traders, and are both fearsome and threatening; the gravity of Mesklin is so high that any object, descending from above, promises instant obliteration; but here towards the equatorial rim, the islanders have developed catapult-launched gliders that can use thermals and counteract the force of gravity. Unfriendly and suspicious, the gliders will block the raft's passage using long, heavy spears to form a barrier through the shallow river-flow.

Eros

Who was the Great Ruler, or Great Designer? His identity is a subject of lively debate among historians to this day, all important records of his reign having been obliterated in the Neurological Wars of the 23rd century (Old Earth dating system). (For an excellent popular account of the various theories see *The Great Ruler: Man or Myth* by F. Boyd and H. Dempsey.) All that can be said with certainty is that he became supreme dictator of the old state of North America – and that he devised and put into effect the most grandiose and eccentric early attempt at interstellar colonization.

These were the days before the discovery of a hyperdrive, or even of a method of sub-lightspeed propulsion sufficiently powerful to make interstellar travel practicable. Even a journey to Sol's nearest stellar neighbour, Proxima Centauri, would take five hundred years. Any ship making such a journey would have to be a Space Ark, carrying generations of pioneers who would live and die without seeing their destination: an improbable concept, but one which had been much discussed in primitive visionary literature.

The construction of the ship was the most massive engineering project yet undertaken by humankind, requiring sixty years to complete. The asteroid Eros – cigar-shaped, twenty miles long, swinging in an orbit which periodically brought it close to the Earth – was to provide the shell. Around it grew an enormous manufacturing complex. Living quarters for the construction workers, many of whom would die without ever setting foot on Earth again, were hollowed out of the rock, a network of rooms and corridors which would later house part of the crew. In the centre was a single immense chamber in which the main community would live.

The Great Designer faced one great basic problem. How was it possible to ensure that the remote descendants of the original descendants would be able to bring the mission to a successful conclusion? Indeed, how was it possible to ensure that they would still remember what the purpose of the mission was? The answer, ironically, was to keep the majority of them in complete ignorance.

The ship's passengers were divided into two groups, both genetically manipulated to suit them to their tasks. The crew would carry out the routine tasks of repair and maintenance required *en route*; these required no special intelligence or insight, but rather an unthinking obedience. The perfect models for the crew were found among the ranks of mystics and hermits, people in whom ritual and belief had replaced curiosity and analytical thinking. They never questioned their roles, but revelled in their imagined superiority over the other passengers, whose lives they controlled.

Inside the ship was a complete miniature world, consisting of a small valley bounded by apparently impassable mountains. The ship's rotation produced normal gravity for the valley's inhabitants, who had no idea that they were in the middle of a journey, let alone that their whole environment was an ingenious hoax – that the 'sky' above their head was actually the far wall of the ship, and that the historic accident which was said to have walled them into their valley was part of the sham.

But curiosity was not part of their normal make-up. In fact they were placid, obedient – even a little stupid. Their civilization was based on that of the Aztecs of Mexico, a timeless agrarian way of life with the populace kept under control by a savage religion. They were not actually Aztecs. In fact they were carefully selected from all parts of the world and carried within themselves the genes which ultimately would produce the exceptional intelligence their colonist descendants would need to survive on a new world. But genetic engineering had made that intelligence recessive and the docile, bovine qualities dominant. Two such groups were bred, with slightly differing genetic make-up. When they met and intermarried the recessive genes would become dominant and their children would be geniuses. While they kept apart they remained dull primitives.

Enforcing this separation was easy. Each group lived in its own village, separated by a river that ran the length of the valley. Intermarriage was forbidden under threat of dire punishment by their terrible gods. One of those deities – the frightful serpent-headed Coatlicue – roamed the valley at night, ready to tear the living heart from anyone found outside the safety of their own village. They were not to know that 'Coatlicue' was actually a Heat-Seeking Robot programmed for this very task.

Thus five hundred years of slow travel passed. The villagers' numbers were kept under control by periodic infestations of poisonous snakes (released by the watching crew). They waited for the day, promised by their religion, when they would be freed from their confinement. Insane as it was, the project might have succeeded had not the crew become obsessed with their mission.

This was where the Great Ruler's plan failed. Over the centuries the crew's roles became more and more ritualized. They formed a quasi-religious hierarchy, with the humble Watchman at the bottom and the Master Observer becoming a sort of high priest at the top. There grew up the millenarian cult of the First Arriver – the first genius-level offspring of the valley, whose appearance would presage the end of the journey. But they forgot that the responsibility for finding a suitable planet and

Coatlicue *(overleaf)*
The fearsome Coatlicue robot stalks the marshes of the valley between dusk and dawn, programmed to seek out and destroy any creature of human size found outside the villages during these hours. Its sophisticated sensors enable it to detect heat sources from considerable distances. In the distance the step-pyramid temple of Quilapa village looms, scene of hundreds of bloody ritual sacrifices by the Aztec priests who, with the threat of Coatlicue to back them up, keep the populace under tight control.

The Valley (previous page) From a vantage point high above the Valley the pronounced curvature of the small world can clearly be seen. A river runs the length of the Valley, providing a natural barrier between the two primitive communities. The Valley's 'sun' is actually a ball of plasma in a controlled fusion reaction; it runs across the 'sky' (whose illusion of reality is complete even at close proximity) on tracks. Here, having finished its daily traverse of the sky, the sun is about to enter the interior of the asteroid, where it will cross under the Valley in time to emerge above the distant mountains for tomorrow's dawn. Night is about to fall: in the Valley the villagers hurry to the safety of their villages as Coatlicue emerges to stalk the fields and marshes.

accomplishing landfall was theirs. When the ship arrived in the Proxima Centauri system they decided, as a matter of faith, that none of the planets was habitable. 'If the planets were suitable He (the Great Designer) would not have given us a choice', said their central doctrine. So a new course was set for another system.

Perhaps thirty years later the fragile equilibrium of the valley was, inevitably, broken. A couple from different villages became lovers, and in due course a child was born who was to discover the secret of his world and, reversing the ship's course, set it on course for its eventual destination, the fourth planet of the Proxima system.

Now, of course, the spaceship, still in orbit around Chimal (the world named for that first genius child), is a popular museum, visited by thousands each year. Yet few of those who walk vertiginously on its 'sky', or queue up to let their children ride on the shoulders of the robot Coatlicue, realize just how extraordinary its history really is.

Arrakis

Arrakis, third planet of the star Canopus, is perhaps the harshest environment ever colonized and (to a degree) mastered by mankind. Its popular name tells us why: *Dune*, desert planet. Between the latitudes of 60°N and 70°S stretches nothing but deep desert, totally inhospitable; this is the Great Flat. The polar ice caps are tiny, in keeping with the central fact of life on Arrakis: water, or rather the absence of it. Forming a partial ring around the North Pole are the mountain ranges known as the Shield Wall and False Wall, rising to a maximum height of 7,400 metres (Mount Idaho). Around the mountains protected from the full force of sandstorms which may reach 700 kph are clustered the human communities: the cities of Arrakeen and Carthag (the former the traditional seat of government, the latter developed by the Harkonnen family during their tenure), and the villages of the imperial subjects. These habitations are centred on the Imperial and Hagga Basins, the most hospitable parts of this arid world. Although the Empire nominally controls Arrakis, it is only in these small areas that its rule is actually effective. Elsewhere, the only human beings to be found are the 'natives', the Fremen.

Fremen The *Imperial Dictionary* defines the word as meaning 'sand pirate', reflecting the reputation for fierceness and lawlessness which these hardy people, who bow to no Emperor, have acquired. They are actually the descendants of the Zensunni Wanderers, a late Mohammedan sect, somewhat reactionary in nature. They settled on Arrakis, where conditions reflect (though with enormously greater intensity) those in the terrestrial deserts where their distant ancestors lived. Like their ancestors they have become masters of their environment. Their society is centred − fanatically and necessarily − around the conservation of water. It is reflected in language as well as in custom. The instruction, 'Get his water!', issued by a Fremen leader, is an order to kill. Corpses (which are 70 % water) are invariably recycled; nothing is wasted. The phrase is not a euphemism. Human life is cheap in the harsh environment of Arrakis, while water is infinitely the most precious commodity on the planet; the instruction reflects these priorities.

The Fremen are fearsome warriors, honed by their way of life to a peak which no conventional soldier − even the Emperor's elite Sardaukar corps − could match. Their preferred weapon is the *crysknife*, a double-edged blade, milk-white in colour and about 20 centimetres long. Crysknifes are manufactured by grinding down the teeth of the sandworm (see below) and will disintegrate, unless specially treated, if not kept in

Arrakeen *(overleaf)*
The old city of Arrakeen is the traditional centre of planetary government. Here, on the landing field, a party emerge from the administration building to board an ornithopter − one of the insect-like flying machines commonly used for transport. In the foreground stands a Fremen, dressed in the close-fitting stillsuit which minimizes water loss.

close proximity to a human body.

The Fremen live in cave systems (erosion is, obviously, a major force on Arrakis) known as *sietches*. The name originally denoted a place for meeting in times of danger, but conditions on Arrakis, where danger is omnipresent, soon led to its adoption as the term for Fremen homes. A large sietch may accommodate several thousand Fremen, while remaining hidden to the outside world. Entrances are sealed off by rock plugs which are both an aid to secrecy and a protection against water loss. Water for the sietch is obtained by the use of windtraps, devices which make use of temperature drops within them to precipitate out the fractional amounts of moisture carried by winds. It is then stored in pools within the sietch, protected by rock walls from the depredations of sand trout (see sandworm).

To an offworlder a Fremen sietch – a place of dimly-lit tunnels opening out into shadowy caverns – might seem primitive and claustrophobic, but their mere existence as havens of relative peace and comfort is testimony to humanity's ability to adapt to the most hostile environments.

Stillsuits In the open desert an unprotected man might lose up to five litres of water per day – a level of dehydration quite inconsistent with the need to conserve every possible molecule of water. Thus the Fremen have devised the stillsuit, a highly efficient device for minimizing water loss. A stillsuit consists of a number of layers. The innermost is porous allowing perspiration to pass through it. The next two layers precipitate salt, and the reclaimed water circulates to containers ('catchpockets') by osmosis and the pumping action of bodily movements. It can then be drunk through a tube. Waste matter is processed in thigh pads. Nose and mouth filters prevent loss of moisture through breathing. A stillsuit in proper working order can reduce water loss to a couple of cubic centimetres a day (mostly through the palms of hands, which can be protected by gloves when not being used to work). It is a marvel of efficient, practical engineering. A stilltent offers similar protection to one or more Fremen required to spend the night in the desert.

Sandworm It seems almost impossible that a planet such as Arrakis could maintain a native ecology, but not only does it do so, it produces the largest creatures known anywhere in the galaxy: the Sandworm, or Shai-Hulud. No one knows just how large a sandworm may grow, but certainly they may attain a length of 400 metres. For all their size they have immensely delicate senses, being able to detect movement on the sand from large distances. Thus the open desert is a dangerous place to travel. Water is poisonous to the sandworm, and they never venture within a certain distance of the poles. They are virtually invulnerable when fully-grown: the only known way of killing one (short of a nuclear explosion) is to apply a powerful electric shock separately to each of its many segments, thus electrocuting it by stages.

For all its size, the sandworm generally feeds on the tiniest of creatures – the sand plankton, which are themselves the first stage of the worm's life cycle. There are three stages in the life of shai-hulud: sand plankton, sand trout (or 'Little Maker') and sandworm. The sand trout are small leathery creatures, roughly diamond-shaped, a few centimetres on a side. They have no apparent sensory apparatus, but are able to detect water at considerable distances (in porous rocks etc). In the deep sand they link together – using cilia along the sides of their bodies – and form a kind of sack around the water, thus providing protection to any nearby sandworms. Next, from the water mixed with the sand trout's excretions, the fungoid growth known as the 'pre-spice mass' forms. Eventually a giant bubble of carbon dioxide forms as a by-product of the process and 'blows' the pre-spice mass to the surface. Most of the sand trout are destroyed in the process; a few survive to enter an encysted hibernation stage from which they emerge, six years later, as sandworms. Of these, yet more will be eaten by full-grown worms or poisoned by water pockets. A very few attain maturity. On the surface the pre-spice mass becomes *melange* (see below), to be scattered about the desert through the movements of sandworms. The melange provides food for the microscopic sand plankton, which in turn (if they survive the sandworms' depredations) grow into sand trout.

The sandworm is the master of Arrakis – but not of the Fremen. They have learned to ride the worms in order to travel swiftly across the desert. Normally a sandworm stays beneath the surface, but the Fremen use a pair of hooks to hold open the front edge of a ring segment, preventing the worm from burrowing (if it tried to do so sand would penetrate its sensitive interior). The Fremen sandrider summons a worm by use of a thumper (a device which beats regularly on the sand to attract the worm's attention). Standing to one side like a skilled bullfighter he catches hold of a ring segment with his hooks. The worm rolls to keep sand out of the opened segment, and the rider is brought around to stand on its back. By skilled use of the hooks sandriders can steer the worms, which can be ridden to exhaustion.

Spice factory (*overleaf*)
A spice factory at work, harvesting the valuable melange spice from the desert sand. The sand is sucked in at the front, the spice is extracted in centrifuges, and the used sand is then ejected at the side. An ornithopter in the foreground gives an impression of the factory crawler's size. Big as it is, however, it is vulnerable to a large sandworm and constant aerial vigilance must be maintained while the factory is at work.

Melange Arrakis would be an unimportant backwater of the Empire were it not for this one product. Melange – commonly known simply as 'spice' – is its sole export, but it is a substance of almost incalculable value elsewhere in the galaxy. This by-product of the sandworm's life-cycle has unique properties when imbibed by humans. Firstly, it is the only known method of retarding the ageing process. Secondly, it is used by Spacing Guild navigators as an aid to their work, as it can produce apparently prophetic visions. The Fremen use melange extensively. The visible evidence for this is their eyes: spice addiction turns both whites and pupils a deep blue colour.

Melange is harvested by large factories. They are delivered to the vicinity of spice patches by extra-large ornithopters, which then stand by to lift off the factory when – as inevitably happens sooner or later – a sandworm appears. For large as the factories are (120 metres long and 40 across) a fully-grown shai-hulud can swallow one whole.

(from Dunn's Cosmic Gazetteer, 17th ed.)

Ringworld

Truly one of the wonders of the galaxy, the Ringworld is by far the largest artificial object known to mankind. Statistics can hardly begin to convey the immensity of this colossal planet. Its radius is over ninety million miles, its circumference about six hundred million miles, the width of the ring one million miles. Its total surface area is some three million times that of the Earth. Its atmosphere is retained by thousand-mile high mountains at the rim. To cross the floor of the Ringworld would be equivalent to circling the Earth forty times, while to circumnavigate it would take nearly an hour travelling at the speed of light.

Yet for all its size, the Ringworld's mass is little more than that of the planet Jupiter. Its manufacture must have been an epic endeavour. Using techniques we can only guess at, the humanoid Ringworld Engineers swept its solar system (that of the star EC-1752) clean of solid matter, transmuting much of it into the super-strong foundation material which keeps the ring from tearing itself apart under its rotational velocity of 770 miles per second. It was vital that no other solid material be left in the system, as any collision with the Ringworld might puncture its floor, allowing its atmosphere to escape in an unstoppable gush. (In fact such a collision did occur, with a wandering object from outside the Ringworld system, but fortunately for its inhabitants the foundation material stretched far enough before fracturing that the hole was above the level of the atmosphere. The mountain thus formed, Fist-of-God, is illustrated on pages 82-83.)

Why was such a vast engineering project necessary? The answer is simply that for all their sophistication in other technology the Ringworld Engineers never discovered the principle of faster-than-light travel. Their empire grew to encompass ten worlds; even to visit half of them would take one of their slower-than-light ramships twenty-four years subjective time – several hundred years elapsed time on one of the worlds. The Ringworld provided them with almost infinite space for expansion, all of it within ten days' travel (using their high-speed transportation system: a linear accelerator running along the top of the rim). When the project was completed, the population of all ten worlds moved to their new home.

We can only guess at the glories of the Ringworld civilization at its height. Unlimited power was available, generated on the so-called shadow squares (which provide night and day to the planetary surface) and beamed down. The power of transmutation meant that any element was available in abundance. Only a few examples still remain of their floating cities (such as the Dream Castle, pictured on pages 86-87), and these are impressive enough. But perhaps, like the Parthenon or Stonehenge on Earth, the

Approaching the Ringworld (*overleaf*)
A spaceship nears the Ringworld. It is too far away to pick out any details, but the Ringworld surface can be seen clearly, divided into sections of night and day by the immense shadows cast by the Shadow Squares which circle the system's sun in a closer orbit. Each of the Shadow Squares is 2½ million miles long and a million miles across; they are kept in formation by threads of an ultra-strong wire.

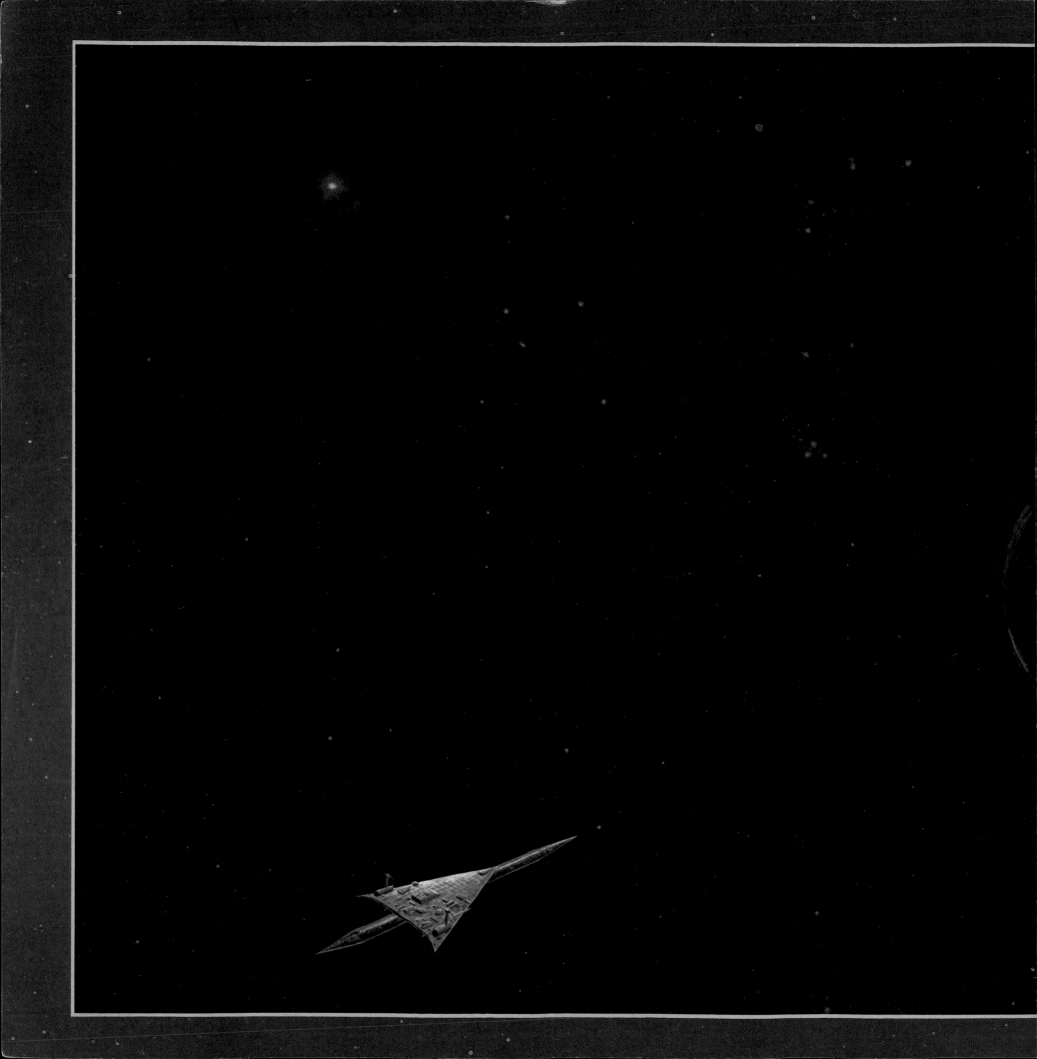

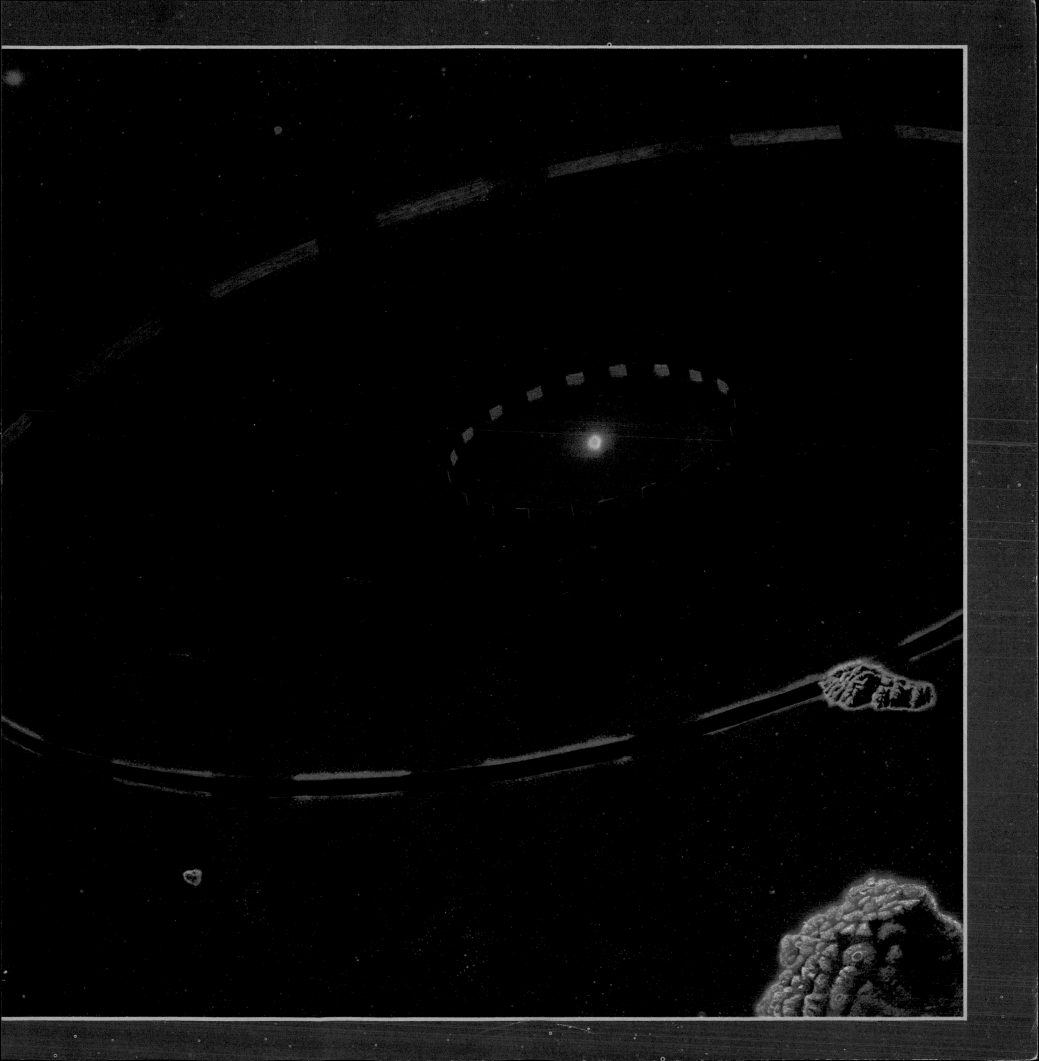

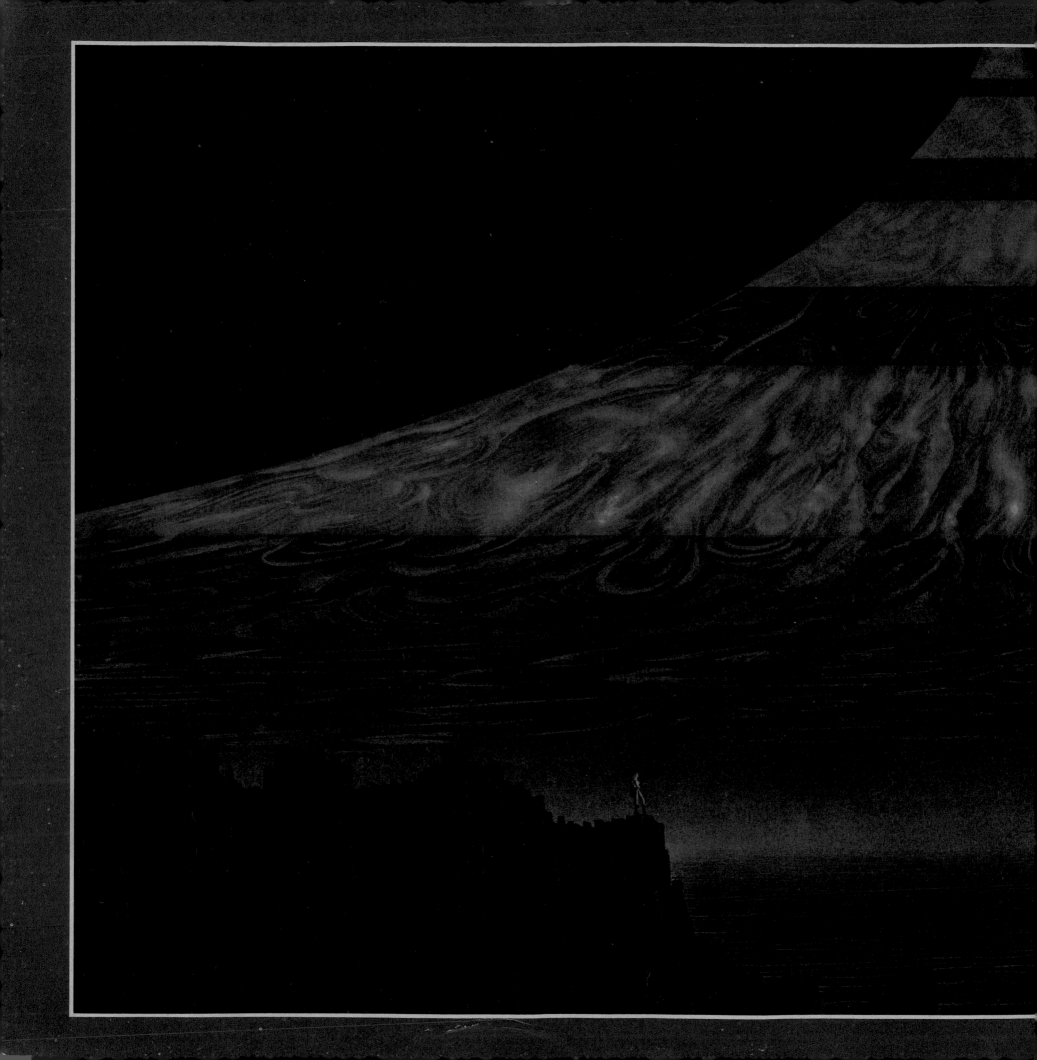

Ringworld Surface at Night *(previous page)*
Only at night can the true awesomeness of the
Ringworld be appreciated on its surface. In
daylight the landscape dwindles away into a
hazy, horizonless infinity; at night the arch of
the Ringworld becomes visible, soaring
overhead – a mere line of brightness at its
apex – and descending again at the other side
(behind the vantage point of this picture). At
night it is possible to appreciate the sheer
immensity of the Ringworld. The mountain
in the right foreground is the thousand-mile-
high Fist-of-God, formed by the impact of a
massive meteorite striking the underside
of the Ringworld and causing even the
fantastically strong foundation material to
bulge inwards.

Ringworld achieves greater magnificence in its partially ruined state than it would have done when whole.

How did such a mighty civilization fall, and why did it descend so quickly into barbarism? (It is estimated that the fall took place only some 1500 years before the first exploration team landed on the Ringworld.) The answer is simple, and a warning to any civilization not to become overdependent on advanced technology. Naturally enough, the Ringworld Engineers took pains not to take to their new home undesirable organisms, such as harmful bacteria; the Ringworld was to be a true Utopia, free of damaging influences. However, their home worlds were not completely emptied in one go, and ramships continued to visit them in search of forgotten items which formed part of their heritage. Such a ramship – or perhaps many of them, over a period of years – brought back to the Ringworld the seemingly insignificant substance which was to bring about its collapse – a species of mould. This mould was able to destroy the structure of a superconductor widely used in Ringworld machinery. We do not know how long it was before its action became apparent, but we can infer that it was slow enough that by the time any alarm was raised the mould had spread the length and breadth of the Ringworld. There were two devastating consequences. The first was that the power beam receivers broke down, bringing about the catastrophic Fall of the Cities in which all the floating buildings, excepting the few with independent power sources, fell out of the sky, destroying themselves and smashing the buildings beneath them. There was heavy loss of life.

Disastrous though this was, the Ringworld might have recovered had the *cziltang brone* not been disabled by the mould. The *cziltang brone* was the device the Ringworld Engineers used instead of an airlock to allow access from the inner surface of the planet to the outer surface where the spaceports were sited. It made the material of the planet permeable, so that it was possible, with slight difficulty, to walk through it. It was safer than an airlock – in the event of a breakdown an airlock might leave air leaking out of the Ringworld, whereas the *cziltang brone* would only leave a solid floor of ring foundation material – but once it was inoperable there was no way of leaving the Ringworld's surface until it was repaired.

Thus the Ringworld Engineers found themselves caught in a subtle trap of their own making. Without power they could not develop new superconductors; without access to their spaceports they could do nothing to restore their power supply. Their transmutation machinery was inoperable; what metal they had was already in use in machinery. They could not dig for ore, as they might have done on a natural world: all that lay beneath their feet was a layer of soil covering the ring foundation material.

Still, all might have been saved had the Ringworld maintained an adequate supply of stored power. But it did not, and such power that was still available was wasted in keeping 'essential' services working. And so the opportunity was lost and its civilization reverted to primitive levels, the half-remembered builders worshipped as gods.

The Ringworld was discovered in about 2800 by the Pierson's puppeteers, whose flight from the explosion of the galactic core (whose wavefront will not reach us for 20,000 years!) took them nearby its star, some two hundred light years from Earth. Their proverbial cowardice made it impossible for the puppeteers themselves to explore the Ringworld, so in order that they could learn more about it (and assess what dangers its inhabitants might pose to their migration), they deputed one of their number, Nessus, to recruit an expedition. Madly impetuous by their standards, unbelievably timorous by our, Nessus enlisted two humans and one kzin as crew; the famous team of Louis Wu, Teela Brown, Speaker-to-Animals and Nessus duly made the trip to the Ringworld. The prize, for human and kzin alike, was the secret of the puppeteers' improved hyperdrive.

Approaching the Ringworld, they were shot down by its automatic anti-meteor defences and made a crash landing on the planetary surface in the vicinity of Fist-of-God. Their adventures on the Ringworld are chronicled in Larry Niven's definitive history. During their travels they encountered one of the few surviving original Ringworld Engineers, Halrloprillalar Hotrufan, who had been among the crew of a ramship which had been making a trip when the collapse happened, and had returned to find it already part of history. They had improvised a temporary *cziltang brone* in order to get back to the planet's surface; it had later failed, denying them escape. From her testimony, together with the deductions of Nessus and Louis Wu, this fragmentary history of the Ringworld is derived.

(from *Artificial Worlds in Fact and Fiction* by L. Van Cott, published by TransGalactic Viewbooks Ltd, Trantor, 26680 New Universal Era)

Dream Castle *(overleaf)*
The Dream Castle, one of the few remaining reminders of the glory of Ringworld civilization at its zenith. Once the skies above Ringworld cities must have been filled with these immense structures, floating with the help of power beams from the surface. When the civilization collapsed and the power failed all except a few, like this one, with self-contained power sources fell ruinously to the ground. The shattered remains of the city stretch for miles on the surface. Approaching the Dream Castle can be seen three of the vehicles used by the Louis Wu Exploration Team.

Trantor

Suggested reading

1. *Artificial Worlds in Fact and Fiction* by L. Van Cott, published by TransGalactic ViewBooks Ltd., Trantor. N.U.E. 26680

2. 'Centralisation of Imperial Government as a Causative Factor in Population Unrest during the First Galactic Era', from *The Decline and Fall of Trantor* (symposium) published by Edwards Literary Empire Ltd., 29997 Gal. Era.

3. 'Effect on Information flow through Administrative channels on Trantor of Revisal of Trade Routes during period of Peripheral Unrest N.U.E. 24457', *ibid.*

4. *Encyclopaedia Galactica*, 24000th edition (903 vols), pub. Terminus-Galactic HoloBooks Inc.

5. *Dunn's Cosmic Gazetteer*, 45th edition published 28891 N.U.E. by Pierrot-Galactic Information Publishing Ltd., Venuria

6. *Beneath the City's Skin*, an account of the subterranean technology of Trantor by R-Petr Lor. Published by Imperial University Press in association with Robot Art Ltd. N.U.E. 25596

7. *Foundation and Empire* (novel) by Isaac Asimov. Galactic Press edition published 24443 N.U.E. First published year 7 Atomic Era.

8. *The Lost Administrator's Office*, and other folk tales of Trantor, published by Robstok Galactic HackBooks Ltd. 22323 N.U.E.

The history of the planet Trantor is the history of an Empire. During the twelfth and thirteenth millennia of the Galactic Empire it was commonly known that 'all roads lead to Trantor', the world that was the social and administrative centre of the Galaxy. For more than two thousand years Trantor was unarguably the most important planet in the enormous Empire of Man, a Federation of more than 25 million populated worlds whose affairs, progress, well-being and punitive sanctions were watched and controlled from this 'single, gleaming Imperial earth'.[1]

Trantor had just one function: Administration. It had just one purpose: Government. And it had just one manufctured product: Law. Trantor was at the very centre of the Empire and it drew for its strength upon the Empire, waxing and waning with the Empire, and when the Imperial dynasty began to fall, not surprisingly Trantor declined soon after. There are historians who believe that it was Trantor that fell first, and that the decline of the first Empire was caused by that fact. This matter is in dispute.[2][3]

Situated close to the Galactic Centre, Trantor was an Earth-type world of a brilliant yellow-white sun; in this region of space the stars burn so brightly that the distinction between night and day is small – this is thought to have been the major factor in causing the population to build an 'artificial' sky, enclosing themselves ever more deeply in an environment where they might control the light. Not surprisingly, bearing in mind the particular surface features of Trantor during the First Empire, the world was unobservable from space, shining too brightly for the naked eye.

It is thought that Trantor began as an ordinary colonized world, with a number of city-installations built as convenient locations across its surface, most of them close to the several small oceans of the world. Its selection as the main Administrative planetary 'bureau' probably occurred during the late seventh, or early eighth millennium of the Galactic Empire.[4] Thereafter, because of its convenience in relation to the bulk of the 25 million worlds, its importance rose and the amount of information stored upon, and cycled through Trantor became overwhelming. More and more cities were built, each with a designated Galactic sector under its control, and more and more of the land resources were mined to give materials for building. By the early twelfth millennium Trantor had long been a single, enormous planet-wide city, a metal covered world supporting a still-rising population of forty billions. The land area of Trantor was 75 million square miles, and of all this only one hundred square miles remained as it had been originally, an area of green in the desert of metal; this, of course, was the garden area of the Imperial Palace.[5]

This meant that Trantor was totally dependant upon imports, a fact that made the world fatally vulnerable during the fall of the First Empire. But whilst it was active, Trantor was supplied by the entire agricultural production of 20 nearby agricultural worlds; two entire worlds were set up to administrate the supplies to Trantor; local industrial worlds regarded Trantor as their main supply of exports; the tourist trade to Trantor was the highest in the Galaxy, and before the discovery of the gigantic artificial worlds, Trantor was retrospectively regarded as the seventeenth Wonder of the Galaxy. Water was the only natural product that Trantor could supply for itself, tapping subterranean reservoir systems, and purifying the oceans; water was stored in vast underground tanks, and purified after use through the hydroponic farming systems in the deep levels. Hydroponics on Trantor were developed to an immensely sophisticated level, thus giving the world a measure of self-sufficiency, but certainly not enough to maintain its vast population.

Surprisingly, the city over Trantor rarely rose above the height of 500 feet from the original ground level. In the late twelfth millennium, for example, the Luxor Hotel at 500 feet above ground level gave a panoramic view of the metal skin, the ever-increasing complexities of man-made structures, the endless horizon of metal against sky, stretching out to almost uniform greyness so that even the hundreds of hotels and landing ports and over-city airways, with their moving taxis and traffic, became a blur.

What was often forgotten was that Trantor extended over a mile *below* the surface, with levels, streets and whole 'open' areas, lit by artificial suns and given an artificial climate.[6] The subterranean city extended below the beds of the small oceans – which in any event were practically hidden by wave-energy and element/water extracting technology – and shafts were also sunk so deep into the crust that the vast temperature differences of the world could be tapped to supply all the energy the lower city required. The upper city was mainly solar-powered. Certainly fusion-generated energy (atomic) became obsolete on Trantor long before it became obsolete on other technologically advanced worlds.

Legal system on Trantor Because the Emperor was situated on Trantor – and part of the Imperial family always in residence there – Trantor naturally became the planet of Appeals, the justice centre of the Galaxy, and the location of some of the most spectacular and important trials in Galactic History.[4] It is not surprising to learn that

View from the top of the Luxor Hotel, Trantor *(overleaf)*
The planet Trantor is a single city; practically every square mile of its land surface is covered by buildings, by metal, by the artificial skin that makes Trantor gleam so brilliantly beneath its young yellow sun. The view from the top of Trantor's highest building, the Luxor Hotel, is the first stop for every tourist. It is the high point of any visit to the world. The view shows some of the most famous buildings in the Galaxy, beginning with the oblong colossus that is the InterStel Building (left), the centre for the Galaxy's most profitable spaceline; next to it rise the hemispheres of the Trantor Opera House, which apart from its regular programme, gives daily matinee performances of the Empire's most popular musical, *Hari Seldon: Superstar.* In the foreground rises the sombre shape of the Public Law Courts, rank upon rank of Judicial Chamber and Public Gallery; next to it, the transparent hemisphere of an Upper Park, a sprawling recreation facility for those who live and work on Trantor. One of Trantor's many film studios can be seen on the right, standing before the nearest of the archaic signal towers; this studio is Tran-Capellan HolVision.

1988 GE   TRANTOR   10 CR

IMPERIAL NEWS

TIME CRIMES TRIAL
EVIDENCE OVERWHELMING

FaxHol transmission from
Legal Correspondent

In the Imperial High Council today the prosecution of Charal Palat and Robert Carlsen for crimes against the code of Time Breaching reached its dramatic peak. The Lord Prosecutor of the Committee of Public Safety, Pitr Wistonia, presented the final pieces of evidence that should ensure the conviction of the two off-worlders for Time Breaching, and earn their physical displacement.

Throughout the long second session the Chief Commissioner Irak Cheon, and the Observer from the Wall of Years (representative of the Time Corps) sat impassive and immobile, their eyes fixed on the shaking defendants.

Palat and Carlsen are charged in that between the years 26687 and 26687 of the New Universal Era (11784th year et seq of the old Galactic Era) they abused the facilities of the Space-Time Research and Control Building on the forbidden world of Necronomicon 7 (Delphinus Sector) and made four personal time-space flux controlled visits to the early nuclear age of earth. The pleas are Only Slightly Guilty (Palat), and Reduced Responsibility (Carlsen).

The core of the evidence is the appearance 1) in works of fiction and 2) as colour artwork wrapped around certain ancient printed papers called *magazines*, of alien life forms, space ship designs and planetary views that could not possibly have been known before the major expansion period into the Galaxy. The first dramatic evidence was the detailed description of the alien artefact known as Orbitsville which was printed in fictional form in the early nuclear age. The Prosecutor pointed out that Palat had been in the initial exploration team of the artefact whilst undertaking his Federation Space Service.

The defence council, StarLord Graar Jarnox, argued that the existence and form of an Orbitsville could have been deduced from the available technology and math of the nuclear age. This was shouted down and the score advanced one point in favour of displacement.

The court was then shown the most dramatic piece of evidence yet produced, the picture of a magazine dated 1949 in old calendar, thought to refer to the terrestrial years subsequent to the first appearance of the Christlord. The magazine, called *Superscience Stories* as far as the translator could determine, showed a fully detailed and accurate representation of a dorgan, the intelligent life form of the planet Cepheus C4. The defence argued coincidence. The Prosecutor then drew the council's attention to the small human figure in the picture, which was unmistakably a depiction of the defendant Carlsen. Other magazine evidence included a painting of the entire range of ThruSpace Cargo and Passenger Liners still in operation as an independent company, and painted thousands of years before by the artist Paul.

In his address to the public, Prosecutor Wistonia drew attention to the fact that it was not the specific examples of time-information-transference (breach of the T.I.T. code) that were important, but the principle of non interference that was being threatened. Time agents were hard at work across a span of years from the early Stone Age of Earth to the time in the future when the Universal structure was so unstable, relatively, that there was an effective barrier to further travel. They worked constantly on their programme of assassination, fund-switching and technological frustration in order that specific catastrophes might be averted. The presence of Carlsen in mid-nineteenth century America had led not only to the premature development of the striptease, but also to the development of the photon bomb, and its use in 1915 to destroy Germany, and half of the surrounding continent of Europe. A single bedroom assassination had averted that, but it was still unsure as to whether or not any long term trends had been instigated by the defendants.

The verdict is expected tomorrow, but already StarLord Jarnox has lodged an appeal against it, claiming that a transtemporal reporter had leaked the result seventeen years ago. He quoted from the statement made by Palat on his arrest: 'My life would have been completely different had I not known that I would be executed for time crimes!'

Strike Causes Fuel Delay

FleetFax transmission from
Federation Offices on Darkover

Unofficial action by ferry crew in the four world system of Alpha Lyris seriously interrupted the transportation of 2000 units of the precious fuel 'firestone', exported by the planet Pern, and due to be delivered to Cowper's World (Alpha Lyris 2) by the end of the Galactic month.

Cowper's World imports over 8000 units of this short-lived and essential fuel every Trantorian year, in exchange for the precious fungicidal crystals mined from its own barren crust. By a-Lyrisian law if an import decays for any reason at all the loss must be borne by the exporting world. The ferry crew's action is because of the failure of their employer, InterWorlds Freight Shuttle and Postal Services Ltd. to pay danger bonuses during periods of peak solar flare activity. Alpha Lyris is still burning hydrogen, but is beginning to redden, and the surface activity has increased noticeably during the last millennium.

Discovery of Generation Ship

Age of Galactic Man pushed back to earliest date

Holofax transmission from our
Science Correspondent, Demon Maurice

The discovery of generation ship 'Suzie', drifting at 0.1C between the Galactic Spiral Arms in the region of magnetic isolation known as Old Duval's Gorge, has upset current theories that Galactic Man only emerged from the Solar System after 3 false starts, the 3 so-called superTechnological ages of Man following the Nuclear Age.

To date, the earliest generation ship discovered was the asteroid 'Eros', now preserved as a museum in orbit around Chimal. Surface features of Suzie have been dated by neutrino-passage-reverberation-decay techniques to the late 19th millenium pre-Galactic time, approximately the 22nd century of the old post-Christlord dating. Automatic messages received from the ship are confirmed as being in the primitive language Swahili, which dominated Earth for more than a millenium. Scientists working on the problem of Galactic man are agreed that Suzie is far earlier than Eros but are split as to whether or not Suzie's primitive ion drive and tungsten hull can be considered as evidence for its departure during the first super technological period. Only if the hull of the ship was opened (a forbidden practice under the new heritage preservation laws) could the vital evidence for Suzie's primary role in the rise of Galactic Man be acquired, namely the extent of chin-regression (nuclear man had a heavy, jutting chin and a tiny pre-frontal lobe) and the extent and colour of body hair.

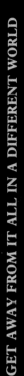

FEATURES INSIDE

Books
— includes a review of Dav Winkrove's new novel of Galactic intrigue in the far future, *Macro Beams against the Ploorans*, plus an extract from the 9000th Jubal Cade western, *Teethmarks in my Horse's Rump*, the continuing story of a gunslinger lost and alone in the High Sierras of Proxima Centauri 7.

My Life with Hari Seldon — the sensational revelations of Seldon's closest friend Gaal Dornick, as related a thousand years ago by Dornick's son's best friend.

And continuing our occasional series on the strangest lifeforms in the Galaxy; this issue: the Vegan Singing Toad (plus songsheets).

FOOTBALL RESULTS

Interplanetary Cup, Second round

Orbitsville Wanderers	Trantor 2-3 Academicals
Sirius Rovers	Red Star 1-1 Mesklin

(full reports on p.24)

Pre-Galactic Man returns

FaxHol transmission from
Culture correspondent

By popular demand the excellent museum display of relics of pre-Galactic man has been brought back to Trantor, and will be open to the public, in the Imperial University, from tomorrow. Among the most exquisite exhibits is a *Russell-Hobbs* steel water container with intact iron electro-conducting filament, circa the second millennium, and a flint knife of the 'polished' kind dating from slightly earlier. The roof and two intact windows of a *voleswakan*, a primitive means of transport, are also on display, with a full scale recon-struction showing how the cater-pillar tracks are believed to have worked. Other exhibits include a steel hip-joint, believed to have been in cosmetic use by the very rich, a rubber-soled boot (dug out of a peat bog) imported from the planet *Poland* (location no longer known) and a very rare matched pair of stylized phalluses, one black and one white, believed to have been used in one of the early risque versions of the game of chess. The pieces were called Bishopricks. The display will be on Trantor for four weeks (Tram-time) and entrance is 10 credits.

New gate to Ree'hdworld

subspaceQuikPrint
from our Technology Editor

His Imperial Highness Hari Gen Chen o'Sulivan travelled into Trantor solar orbit yesterday to officially open the new Stargate to the peripheral stars of the BerSarkan-Mizaria Sector, which supports a hundred colonized worlds and the important human-alien contact zone of Ree'hdworld. Although no colonization traffic is permitted to this particular far-flung world, in view of the delicate nature of the indigenous intelligence, the tourist demand to see the Ree'hd has always been high and the new gate should help considerably with the financing of the poorer worlds in this sector.

The gate, a forty-mile diameter ring of administrative and hotel facilities surrounding the central T-space core of fabric stress, was erected by InstaTrip Pan Galactic Co., based on the standard GravMech thru-space design.

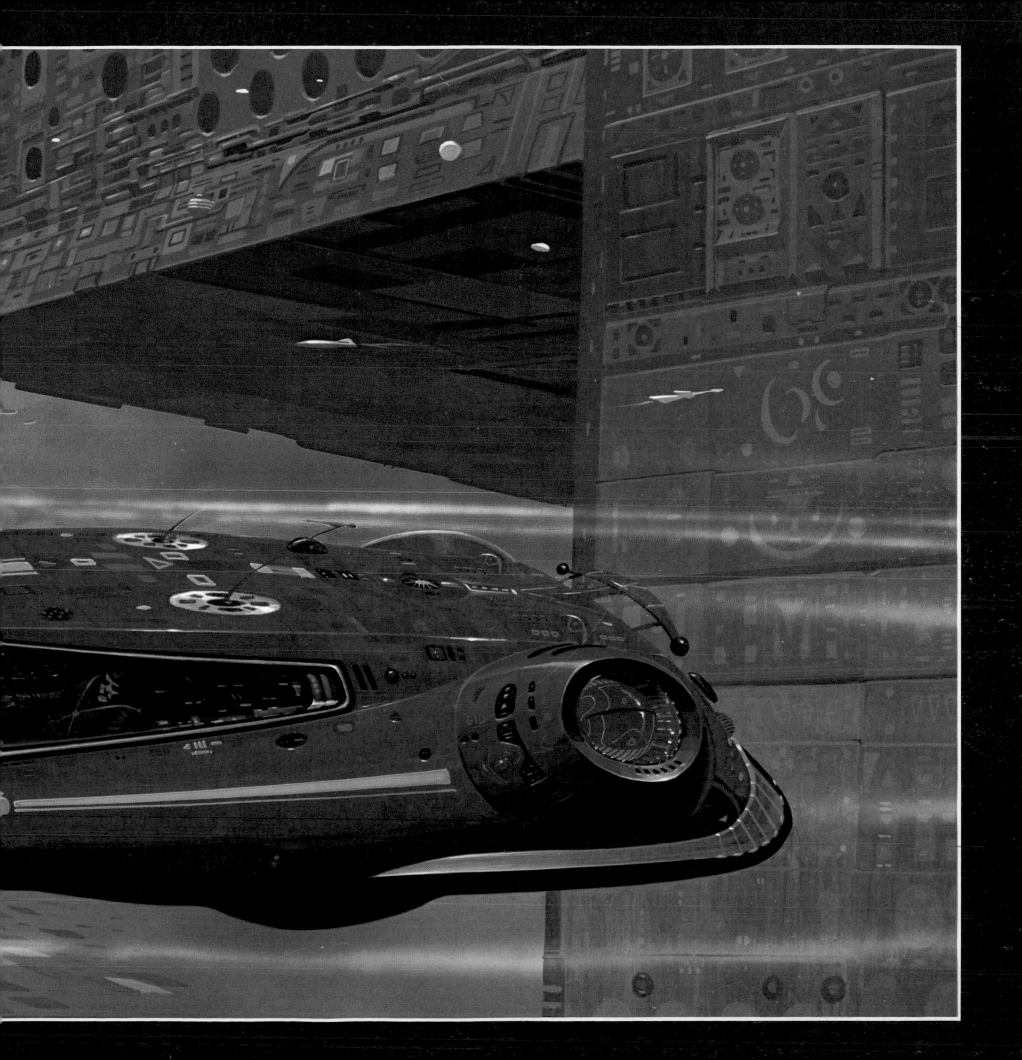

towards the end of the First Empire audiences, and appeals to the Emperor, were never granted; at this time the Imperial family, and Trantor itself, were in the hands of the great aristocratic families, in particular the Chen family, representatives of which formed the Commission of Public Safety, with control over police, armed forces and all public and planetry legal systems. Perhaps the most famous trial at this time was that of Hari Seldon (11988GE-12069) the psychohistorian who was accused of treason when he used mathematics to predict that the Empire would fall within 500 years, and would be followed – unless radical action was taken – by a period of anarchy and 'darkness' lasting 30,000 years. His prophecy, based on the prediction of mass-human behaviour, was treated scornfully by the Commission, and Seldon was found guilty of treason and exiled on the distant planet Terminus.

Seldon's prophesy was to be proved correct, of course. He had seen that as Trantor became more specialized it became more vulnerable and less able to defend itself. And as it became the Administrative centre and Knowledge-repository of the Empire, so it became a greater 'prize'. Imperial succession was becoming more uncertain, and by Seldon's time the Empire was effectively ruled by a number of widespread, powerful aristocratic families whose feuds were already growing more numerous. There was a gradual decline of social responsibility which was just the final straw in initiating the decline of the single, vast Empire. The signs of weakness had been apparent for centuries: the rising bureaucracy, the receding initiative (new-world exploration, for example, was no longer carried on on a large scale with the withdrawal of sponsorship by the Empire), the freezing of caste and the blocking of curiosity. All this Seldon proved could be handled mathematically and used to show, by equation, that change was a certainty, that there would be viceregal revolt – a probably Imperial assassination – and many recurrences of periods of economic depression – this would lead to a dividing of the Empire into many warring States, all growing out of revolution. The accumulated knowledge and order of 12,000 years – now situated on Trantor – would be lost, there would be interstellar war on an unprecendented scale, decay of trade, a decline of population and a communications breakdown on a Galactic scale.

Trantor, it was clear, would be subjected to increasing attack, in order to destroy the Empire at its corrupt heart. Its fall, in the 13th millennium, was brought about by its helplessness, its dependence on imports, and the enormous cost of defending it against attack. Money, poured into the defence of Trantor, was found at the cost of equipping the ships and men of the Empire's armed forces. In war after war they were defeated, until a force of arms came against Trantor that was unstoppable – the so called Great Sack when the mightiest capital in the Galaxy found its powers bent back upon themselves and forever broken.[4]

Life on Trantor continued for thousands of years, but in the trade and communications chaos of the Galaxy, the inhabitants had only two things worth exporting: knowledge, which during the Interregnum was not a valuable commodity; and metal:

In the blasted ruin of death the metal shell that circled the world wrinkled and crumpled into a mockery of its original grandeur. The survivors tore up the metal plating and sold it to other planets in exchange for seed and livestock. The soil was seen again for the first time in millennia, and a primitive agricultural society was established in and among the mighty shards of steel that heaped their massive ruins towards the sky.[7]

The Ruins of Trantor *(overleaf)*
After the Great Sack, when the Empire finally crumbled completely, the function of Trantor as the Administrative Centre of the Galaxy was lost, and its people fell into decay, along with its systems. Once the most magnificent tribute to man's technology, and the most popular tourist planet in the Empire, Trantor now became an embarassment. Layer by layer, level by level, it was torn down, for now it had become the source of another richness: steel. The population that stayed became involved either in the export of the ruined shards of broken buildings, or found a new life for the soil in the rapidly cleared areas of the original planet; they became farmers. Here, with a SolVegan Stripping Freighter winching metal remnants into its cargo hold, is shown the view from the decaying gardens of the Imperial Palace; always built on high ground, the palace looked out across a vista of administrative blocks and huddled population centres. To the right can be seen the immense barrel shape of the shuttle-port for this sector of the world.

Hothouse

The twilight of Earth was a long, seemingly endless period of ages, when an increasingly lush planet basked beneath an increasingly red sun. The period of red cold, when the sun was vast, dim and unable to warm the planet Earth by more than a few degrees, lasted a thousand million years (see *End of the World*). Students of Earth evolution classify the periods of Earth as Rapidly Evolving, Rapid Variform, Consolidation Period, New Evolution, Stable Hothouse and Final Cold. The Stable Hothouse period lasted many millions of years while the sun expanded, reddened and increased in luminosity; it lasted well into the cooling phase. It is of particular interest to cosmologists because of one fact, namely the interevolution of plant and animal life, and the formation of plant intelligence.

By the time Man first appeared on the Earth the biological composition of the world had been in its Consolidation Period for many hundreds of millions of years, the rate of vari-formation slow, although the potential adaptation was still high in the genetic pool. Although man himself tampered with the natural balance of evolution his effect was temporary, and the varieties he induced rapidly went extinct after Earth ceased to be the prime world. This period in the history of Earth concerns us only inasmuch as at this time, and for the ages to come while Sol was still in its active hydrogen-burning phase, the plant kingdom was a passive photo- and geotactic mixture of classes, with only a very few vibration-motivated, animal-eating members (all equipped with particularly powerful digestive juices); parasitism was somewhat more rife, mainly creepers and vines, and a large variety of fungi. Mimicry was almost totally confined to the animal populations, basically cryptic camouflage, the merging in with the background, or mimicking uninteresting plant organelles such as leaves, twigs, or bark. Gradually, as the sun grew redder and larger, and the rotation of the Earth slowed, a dramatic change began to occur across the world.

The New Evolution enhanced the more aggressive survival characteristics of the plant kingdom, perhaps in response to the cutting down of light for photosynthesis, which would have resulted in a desperate struggle to acquire new ways of gaining the energy and protein for growth and propagation. The lush greenness of the canopy, the enormous forest that began to cover the planet, was in stark contrast to the immense dark world below its uppermost branches. Here parasitism, and an almost conscious mobile search for food, became the established pattern of existence, and here too we see the first rudimentary signs of a plant intelligence, evolving, perhaps, out of an increased mimicry on the part of plants that we see continuing apace. But only a fungal form, the *morel*, can be seen to have acquired a true intelligence, based on that recognition-sensitivity known in the ancient world as 'empathy'.

It would be impossible to review fully the variety and extent of the whole of the Hothouse, so we must confine ourselves to a look at some of the more interesting features of it. Which brings up the problem of where to begin, because as with any lush and exotic world, wherever you look you find the unusual, and the weird and the wonderful. But Earth is of interest, in particular, because of the conquest it underwent by a single plant form: the Banyan tree. It is impossible to say when this small, tropical fig tree with its vast rooting branches began to grow and extend, and eventually to propagate in a way that left it in communication with the parent, and slowly, perhaps over a million years or so, came to cover most of the land surface of the Earth. An immense, single tree, stretching hundreds of yards towards the fading sun, and thus forming the middle-ecosphere where practically all life on Earth exists—the sphere of niche and pathway that exists on many levels between the tips of the leaves, and the ground. And only where it approaches the weed-filled salty ocean does this tree hesitate and draw back, and allow glimpses of the majestic, crumbling ruins of Old Earth, the buildings and castles and cities that were long ago overrun, first by creepers, then by plants living *on* the creepers, and then by the Banyan tree itself, spreading out to enfold the ruins. Evidence of 'stone building' man is everywhere to be seen in these beach areas, haunted as they are by such unpleasant life-forms as Killer Willows, and the Sand Octopus, an animal life form that has moved from sea to sandy substratum.

But within that middle ecosphere what an immense variety of vicious life there is. Nettlemoss, Trappersnapper, Pluggyrug, Leapycreeper . . . names that send a shiver through the skin, names that describe so effectively the spreading, questing, prowling plants that share the forest world with man. Oh yes, what of man? If the plants have taken on the aggressive habits of the early animals, then man has taken on some of the features of early plants . . . the greenness of his skin isn't due, as you might be tempted to think, to any chlorophyllic energy production cycle, but is a camouflage, a mimicry. Man lives towards the tops of the tree, using giant nutshells as homes, and the broad palms of leaves as his garden. How many men survive, and live on Old Earth, is impossible to say. But we do know that he lives in friendship with practically none of the plants, and precious little of the animal kingdom. But there are the Termights, one of the last survivors of the insect world, that have achieved a level of intelligence allowing them inter-specific communication. By contrast, Tigerflies, distant relatives

At the Tips; Hothouse *(overleaf)*
A group of humans has made its way to the very top of the forest world, and here there is to be a parting of the ways. The older members of the group are to Go Up, and the younger group, already matured, help them, before leaving to continue their own life deeper in the trees. Gren, one of the younger group, helps Lily-yo, one of the older, into the pod of a Burn-urn plant. The pod is attached to the cable of a traverser, a giant spider-like plant, that spins its web between the Earth and the Moon. When next the traverser sinks to Earth it will pick up the pod and transport it out across the emptiness of space to the lighter world. Whistle-thistles, to the left, and a trappersnapper to the right seem to watch the proceedings; clouds of paperwings flutter about, their colours strangely beautiful to eyes accustomed to monotonous green; in the foliage the beckoning finger of a Black Mouth promises imminent danger.

of the wasp, are confirmed enemies of man: they are narrow waisted, yellow and black armoured creatures, with shaggy hair on the softer parts of their bodies, transparent wings, and long vicious stings; their large, multi-facetted eyes make them excellent hunters, and huge mandibles allow them to gorge even on other armoured creatures.

But it is against the plant kingdom that man, and his animal colleagues and foes, fight the main fight, against such as the Leapycreeper whose roots and stems are also tongues and lashes and which attacks anything, whipping around tree trunks and branches to get at the moving prey . . . especially the Termights. And that Trappersnapper, so difficult to see as its huge, hinged jaws spread wide at the end of its long neck, waiting in the upper foliage for the unwary to be swallowed down, almost to the ground to the huge mouth in its immense vegetable body. Slashweed, with its sword-like leaves giving the human population the sort of duel that their distant ancestors would have known; and the Greenguts and Black Mouth, the former disguising its gaping mouth and stomach as a copse of woods, rod-like trees that can suddenly contract, oozing digestive slime on to the crushed prey; the latter a fleshy black mouth that attracts its prey by singing and beckoning with five chitinous fingers. Then there is the Wiltmilt, a very peculiar adaptation to the Hothouse in that it has evolved–quite independantly of the animal kingdom – an immense, single eye, with a palmate pupil. It is a gigantic plant, able to extend its trunk-like body to the very tips of the trees, or sink down into a squat, bulging mass, its wide vegetable mouth foaming with digestive juices as it seeks its prey by sight.

But the analogous evolution of animal-like optic organs is not the plant kingdom's strangest interaction with the animal world; the fungal intelligence known as the morel, the hunting behaviour of plants, the vast single eyes, all these pale in comparison with the *tummy belly men*. It would be very easy to think of the tummy belly men as man-shaped plants, created in precise images of man, and seen as plants only by their root-like connection with the spiky-leaved, swollen bellied trees known as *tummy trees*. In fact the tummy belly men are real humans, *caught* by the parasitic root extensions which burrow into their backbones and make direct contact with their brains, controlling their actions even as the tree sends nourishing sap down the root to sustain its willing slaves, used to capture the fish and sea creatures on which the tummy trees feed. A symbiotic relationship, then, but rather heavily biased towards the plant.

Symbiosis, parasitism, naked aggression, an exotic and complex ecology contained within the immense span of the single dominating Banyan tree. Man has adapted himself to this seemingly awful life and he survives; he uses shells for his home, and for his protection, he uses dumblers, great fleecy umbrellas with feathered spokes, as parachutes for descending through the Banyan layers; he uses, then, the available resources of the Floran world, and achieves a new balance with nature.

Not everything in the Hothouse world is hostile, and finally, then, we turn to a plant, perhaps the most amazing plant ever to evolve on any world known to man, a plant that has not only mimicked the animal kingdom, but has also found a way of leaving the confines of Earth and spreading its ecological niche as far as the moon. I mean, of course, the Traversers, those immense leguminous spiders that can grow up to a mile in length. Over the millions of years that the radiation of the sun has increased, steadily, inexorably towards that time when it will spit out the last of its heat and light and shrivel up into a white dwarf, during this time the vegetable kingdom has assumed supremacy, overwhelming the Earth and the animal life of the Earth, driving lesser life to extinction or the twilight zone. Surely the Traversers represent the culmination of the supremacy of the plant kingdom, a free-living vegetable form, mimicking the action of spiders in the construction of strong webs not just on the Earth, but between the Earth and the Moon; plant creatures that were able to drift along these ropy ladders through the immense airless cold of space.

from *Homo Botanicus: a Retrospective View of Man's Future*, by Dav belAmi (adapted from the holovision series first shown on Galactic Independent TeleSensation, N.U.E. 25,740)

Catch-carry-kind; Hothouse *(overleaf)*
'I am known as the Sodal Ye, greatest of all Sodals of the catch-carry-kind, Prophet of the Nightside Mountains, who brings you the true word'. The sodal appears to be half fish, half human, its scaly body and tail perched on human-like legs on a boulder, its fish head supporting a hairy, saggy-lipped face. It is friendly, eating gifts brought in the gourds that lie scattered about him. It has set a trap, using the dancing baby, for the intelligent fungus, the *morel*, that is wrapped about the head of the human, Gren; the *morel* has refused to leave the relationship but it wil' go to the younger, healthier child.

End of the World

One of the most popular packages currently being offered by Trans-Temporal Tours is their so-called 'Journey to the End of Time'. Holidaymakers can choose from a range of future eras between 800,000 years in the future and the end of life on Earth countless millions of years hence. People frequently ask if these dramatic scenes truly represent the future destiny of mankind's home world. The answer is that we do not know. Some theories suggest that the future is fixed, immutable, ordained, and that the events we see will inevitably come to pass. Others maintain that there may be many different futures, extending from the present as the branches of a tree extend from its trunk. According to this theory the versions of futurity glimpsed on the tour may come from entirely different branches. But this academic debate is of little concern to the people who crowd to reserve seats on this tour, which in recent years has even outstripped in popularity such perennial favourites as the Crucifixion and the Second San Franciscan Earthquake.

The basic tour takes in four stops:

1. 802,701 A.D. Here we see *homo sapiens* diverging into two related but very different species. On the surface of the Earth live the small, delicate, frail, childlike Eloi. Around them stand the half-ruined, mysterious palaces and statues of a bygone Golden Age (particular landmarks to look for are the white marble statue of a hovering sphinx-like creature – perhaps a representative of an as-yet undiscovered alien species – and the immense, decaying Palace of Green Porcelain). The Eloi themselves have long ago lost the ability to build such monuments. Beneath the Earth, in dark and oppressive tunnels and caverns, dwell the subhuman Morlocks: pallid, ape-like creatures with large reddish eyes adapted to living in their darkened environment. The Morlocks are carnivorous; the Eloi are their prey.

So dismaying is this view of mankind's destiny that some visitors have claimed that the whole scenario is a holovision mockup, and that the entire Journey to the End of Time is a clever sham put together by TTT promoters! This is absurd, of course – and we would caution anyone tempted to test such a theory. The tour will include a stop inside a Morlock cavern, and it is very dangerous to leave the protective field of the Time Machine. The Morlocks are fast and savage, and the Temporal Interference Laws forbid tour guides from retaliation against any which might sieze anyone so foolish as to try! You have been warned!

2. 3500,000,000 A.D. The second stage of the tour takes us to see the final pathetic remnants of mankind on Earth. The scene is impressively desolate. Erosion has reduced most of the land to a bleak moorland. The Earth is moving into another Ice Age, so that even at noon the sun gives out little warmth. No buildings remain: no trace remains anywhere on this world of humanity's achievements. The only creatures to be seen most of the time are small grey animals, halfway between rabbits and kangaroos in appearance, browsing among the patches of grass. Incredible as it may seem, these beasts are the final degenerate descendants of *homo sapiens*. Tourists are also likely to see one of the fearsome predators which, although slow-moving, feed on the grey animals. They are like gigantic centipedes, up to thirty feet in length, their backs protected with thick green-black plates. A human can easily outrun one of these lumbering monsters, but caution is nevertheless advised.

3. 12,250,000,000 A.D. Now the solar system is nearing the end of its life. The resurgence of life during the Hothouse period (not included in this tour) is over; the sun has entered the long twilight period of red cold. The Earth no longer rotates. The Moon is gone. Overhead the sky is black, although the red sun, enormously bloated, sits perpetually on the horizon. We stand by a desolate beach. There are no longer any tides, just a disturbing oily movement of the water which deposits a thick crust of pink salt on the sand. The air is thin; tourists with respiratory difficulties will be issued with breathing equipment by the tour guide. The higher forms of life have disappeared; this period is a distorted reflection of some prehistoric era. The only plants are mosses and lichens, clinging to the rocks. A few insects still live, most notably immense white butterfly-like creatures, but the major forms of life are now crustacea. Giant crabs, their carapaces up to two metres across, roam the beach. They are certainly willing to include human flesh in their diet, so once again care must be exercised.

4. 12,750,000,000 A.D. The final leg of the tour takes us to see the last living creature on Earth. The landscape is even more desolate than before. The only sound is the constant moaning of the wind. The sun barely illuminates the scene with its dark red light. The sea is the colour of congealing blood. At the water's edge we see the last living thing: a tentacled creature, its body a black sphere some twenty centimetres across. At the end terrestrial life has returned to the sea from which it sprang. Soon the world will be as sterile as it was ten billion years ago before the first micro-organisms appeared.

The Time Machine *(overleaf)*
Centuries before modern methods of time travel were perfected one scientific genius, working alone, designed and built the first known Time Machine. This happened in the late Victorian Era on Earth – a scientifically primitive period, when such devices as jet engines and nuclear rockets had only just come into use – in a country called England. Here, thanks to the efforts of a TransTemporal documentary crew, we see the Time Traveller in his laboratory. The Time Machine, a charmingly quaint device of brass, ebony and quartz, stands almost completed, a testament to the inventive power of the human mind transcending technological limitations. By painstakingly filing quartz rods into certain configurations, the Time Traveller managed to duplicate in them the functions of complex solid state circuits used in contemporary time machines. Riding in his Time Machine cannot have been fun; he described the sensation as 'excessively unpleasant. There is a feeling exactly like that one has upon a switchback – of a helpless headlong motion!' Thanks to modern scientific advances, today's time traveller enjoys a far more comfortable ride than this admirable pioneer.

End of the World *(previous page)*
The Time Traveller's explorations took him to
the very end of the world, now the climax of
TransTemporal Tours' popular 'Journey to
the End of Time'. The sun slowly sinks into
extinction, emitting an occasional dying flare.
Its light barely illuminates the landscape. The
Time Traveller stands by the water's edge
watching, to his right, one of the last
remnants of life on Earth: a shapeless,
tentacled creature lying motionless in the
shallows.

Conclusion This is an unusual tour, perhaps not to be recommended to those of a morbid disposition. Nevertheless, from our sample of people questioned 72% thought the holiday excellent and a further 15% said it was very good. Only 2% did not enjoy it. Sample comments included: 'a really unusual experience', 'gave us a whole new perspective on our life situation', 'the most original holiday I've ever had', 'a wonderful source of party conversation'. The only recurring complaint was a tendency to overcrowd the Time Machine, but Trans-Temporal Tours report that with additional trips being laid on in the forthcoming season this problem should not recur. Overall, at 2,450 credits for a 7-day tour, the Journey to the End of Time can be strongly recommended.

(from *Temporal Which?*, N.U.E. 10,724)